then & now

Plymouth - an ever evolving city

written & compiled by

Chris Robinson

edited by

Ben Robinson

PUBLISHING

British Library Cataloguing in Publication Data
Robinson Chris 1954 –
Plymouth Then & Now, photographic comparisons 1860s - 2009
1.Devon. Plymouth, history
1. Title
942.3'58

ISBN 978 - 0 - 9543480 - 7 - 6
Designed By Chris Robinson
Edited by Ben Robinson
© Chris Robinson 2009

First published November 2009

OTHER CHRIS ROBINSON TITLES
PUBLISHED BY PEN & INK

PLYMOUTH AS TIME DRAWS ON – 1985
PLYMOUTH AS TIME DRAWS ON VOL 2 – 1988
VICTORIAN PLYMOUTH: AS TIME DRAWS ON – 1991
PUBS OF PLYMOUTH PAST AND PRESENT
The Harvest Home and one hundred others – 1995
PUBS OF PLYMOUTH PAST AND PRESENT
Prince George and one hundred others – 1997
UNION STREET – 2000
THE ARGYLE BOOK – 2002
ELIZABETHAN PLYMOUTH – 2002
PLYMOUTH THEN & NOW – 2004
IT CAME TO OUR DOOR [revised] – 2005
PLYMOUTH COLLEGE: The First Hundred Years – 2005
THEN & NOW: The Changing Face of Plymouth – 2006
PLYMOUTH'S HISTORIC BARBICAN – 2007
PLYMOUTH IN THE TWENTIES & THIRTIES – 2008
150 YEARS OF THE CO-OPERATIVE IN PLYMOUTH - 2009

Published by
Pen & Ink Publishing
34 New Street
Barbican
Plymouth PL1 2NA
tel; 01752 705337/228120
fax; 01752 770001
www.chrisrobinson.co.uk

Printed & bound in Great Britain by
Latimer Trend & Company Ltd
Estover Close
Plymouth PL6 7PL
Devon

then & now

Plymouth - an ever evolving city

Introduction

In the introduction to the second volume of Then and Now (The Changing Face of Plymouth), we featured the bottom two of the images on this page. Now, of course, the building is finished, fully occupied and named in honour of the man who did so much to put the University in its position of prominence, locally and nationally, Roland Levinsky.

It is a landmark building and one that is visible from all sorts of unlikely angles around the city. The middle view shows the birth of the building, the top view, as it is today. But that too will change, not just in terms of the scenery around it, but also in terms of the physicality of the building itself - the copper cladding will go green over the years with verdigris and this aspect will take on a whole new complexion. Which is precisely why we've opted to call this volume Then & Now Plymouth - An Ever Evolving City.

It's a truism of course, everything changes, nothing lasts forever or stays the same - although clearly some things in life alter more dramatically, more quickly than others.

Take the front cover of the book, for example. There was much debate over whether the changes here, which are mainly peripheral - cars, buses, signage, foliage - merited a front cover billing. Somehow, however, the sheer period quality - and colour - of the Then image sold it. The photograph is also used by Stacey Dyer as a screen saver at the Plymouth Barbican Association's South West Image Bank and has proved very popular with visitors and volunteers there.

Our Editor, Ben, had already taken a Now view for the original article, but when we decided to use it as a cover shot, he went back on a better day and made a concerted effort to not only match the vantage point, but also to try and capture cars and buses in similar positions - a jolly good job he made of it too - thanks.

And then there's his other Now shot of the building we see here, the Levinsky building, on the back cover. This was taken from the Drake Circus complex, just as the earlier one was. There was one significant difference here though, the Drake Circus complex then, in the 1970s was a completely different building to the one that bears that name today, so again trying to match up the images was not easy. However the striking thing about the finished pair is that the new University structure looks, from that perspective at least, like a giant futuristic building from another planet that has just fallen out of the sky and landed here in Plymouth. Is it a sign? Is this the shape of future? Will ever more buildings be erected in Plymouth that don't conform to the traditional square or oblong slab fronted format - I have no doubt they will. The future will also see many taller buildings appear in Plymouth, just hopefully not in our wonderful post-war shopping centre itself! But who knows? Maybe these questions will be partly answered in volume four, whenever that might be ...

Chris Robinson
November 2009

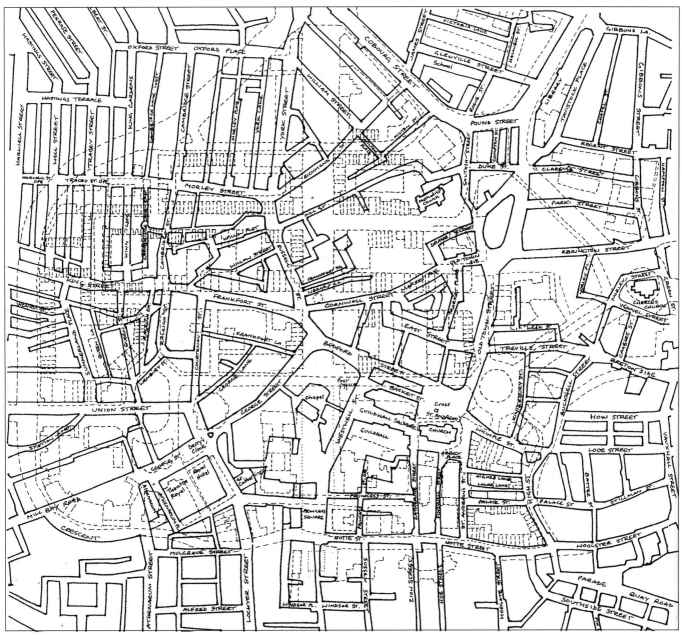

Having spent many hours over the years trying to work out what was where in terms of the pre and post-war city centre I decided to draw up this pair of overlaid maps highlighting, in the one version, the old street pattern and in the other, the modern street arrangement. I used them both for the first time in Victorian Plymouth and again in the previous volumes of Then & Now; and I make no apology for including them here again. They are as useful to me now as they have always been and so I have little doubt that others too will find them helpful, not just in the context of this book, but generally when looking at any old images of the heart of Plymouth.

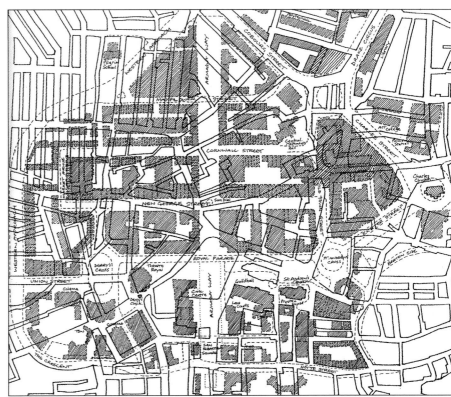

ACKNOWLEDGEMENTS

University site as it appeared in the late-1920, note Public Secondary School under construction, bottom left.

Over the years that I have been taking these Then & Now pairings I have been regularly surprised and delighted to find odd offerings in my Herald mailbag from readers who have taken the time and trouble to put their own 'shots from the same spot' together. I hope I have managed to recall them all, if I've forgotten anyone, please accept my sincere apologies. Similarly if you see a photograph here that you know is yours and yet you have not been credited or consulted, again, I apologise. With so many images coming from so many sources – and with so little information, if anything at all, recorded on the back of them, it is difficult to be as thorough as one would like to be. So thanks to the Herald Library, Plymouth Central Library, Plymouth City Art Gallery and Museum. However the publishers would be happy to hear from anyone who has information concerning the copyright of any uncredited images.

Certainly I know the source of the vast majority of the Now images, for I took them myself, and for anyone who has never tried to make their own Then & Now pairings, I can heartily recommend the practice. It's always a happy challenge to try and find that exact spot that the earlier photographer occupied and it can be an odd sensation when you do think you've found that spot ... you often wonder what that original photographer would have made of the same view today.

And that's an opportune moment to thank all those others who have been recording Aspects of the Evolving City, whether for fun, financial gain or for posterity. So thank you especially Trevor Lear and Derek Carter, both of whom spent sunny Saturday mornings with me, guiding me around Lipson and Laira (Trevor), and Plymstock, Pomphlett, Hooe and Oreston (Derek), armed with their treasured collections of personal pictures. Thanks also to Stacey Dyer and her wonderful team of volunteers down at the South West Image Bank; and to Roy Westlake, Roy Todd, Peter Carlyle, Peter Waterhouse, Peter Taylor, Barry Trevethan, Graham Hobbins, Ken Hopkins, Ron Garratt, Fred Guy, Ern Downey, Dave Luckham, Richard Keoghoe, Sylvia Blott, John Curno, William Gilhen, Bob Cook, Vincent Hart, George Williams and the Plymouth and South West Co-operative. Thanks too to Herald photographers Pete Holgate, Mike Cox, Guy Channing, Tony Carney and many others past and present, similarly to the Herald/Western Morning News editors Alan Qualtrough and Bill Martin.

Thanks to the ever-patient features team at the paper; Su Carroll, Jackie Butler and Martin Freeman. And the even more patient, and long-suffering, Rob Warren and Doreen Mole - the Plymouth Prints team at New Street. To wife and publisher, Clare, for support and proof reading, and to son and editor, Ben. This is the third Then & Now book that Ben has put together and this time he has even more claim to co-ownership of the project than ever before - just days after passing his driving test (September 2009) he set off around Plymouth armed with around thirty Then photographs and came back with some stunning Now images of his own - they are all in the book, and include the marvellous comparison that grace the front and back covers, absolute crackers! So, thanks #2. And to the rest of the family and friends, thanks for just for being there.

Last but by no means least, thanks to Bob Mills, Paul Opie, Dave Manners and Co. at Latimer Trend, who not only do a fine job of printing, but are also extremely understanding, and accommodating, on the deadline front - they had receipt of this copy on 16 November for delivery of books, printed and bound, on the launch date of 27 November 2009. Brilliant! Thanks guys!

Contents

then & now

then & now

Plymouth - an ever evolving city

written & compiled by

Chris Robinson

HOE WATERFRONT

The angles aren't quite right but there's plenty enough scope for comparison and certainly you would be hard pushed to get any other two photographs of the area today that are separated by a greater time period. There's comfortably 130 years between these two images as in our Then snap we look back at Plymouth Hoe before the Belvedere, the construction of Elliot Terrace and the Grand Hotel, before Smeaton's Tower was brought here from the Eddystone Reef, all of which conspire to suggest a date of somewhere around the late-1860s, early-1870s. Note the Then comparatively new Esplanade and Grand Parade developments and the Now very newly completed Azure Building to the west of the Grand Hotel. *H 12 May 2007*

HOE PIER AND BANDSTAND

Curiously enough Plymouth Pier and the Hoe Bandstand were both casualties of the Second World War – but both met their ends in very different ways. The pier was a victim of the 1941 Blitz, its wooden promenade and superstructure surrendering entirely to the flames generated by incendiary devices, while the bandstand was unceremoniously demolished and scrapped for its metal content in the 1942 drive for raw materials that saw ornamental railings and gates of private houses and public buildings removed for the military's melting pot (although many ended up rusting in stockpiles across the country). Happily the little shelters dotted across the Hoe Park survived and are still with us today as, essentially, that fabulous public open space looks much the same as it did when laid out in the 1880s – note however the many changes at West Hoe. *24 Oct 2009*

WEST HOE

The mid-morning sun lights up West Hoe in Barry Trevethan's instantly recognisable shot of the area, while our Now image finds us looking straight into that great ball of fire. More than 50 years separates the two views and yet at first glance they seem so very similar. Clearly what still stands of the grain silo at Millbay no longer cuts the same silhouette against the east Cornwall skyline, the great cranes of Brunel's old Great Western Docks have also disappeared. Meanwhile, in the middle distance one or two of the old West Hoe tennis courts have long since given way to an extremely respectful new development making it more than a little difficult to accurately assess the age of the new apartments. Bizarrely too, it is difficult to date the trees lining West Hoe Park as the trees we see in the Then photograph stand so much taller than their contemporary counterparts. On the waterline itself the Royal Western Yacht Club has long since vacated its home in the little harbour, and has been replaced by the Waterfront bar/restaurant, while the Wet Wok introduced a new gastronomic element into the Hoe foreshore some years ago. *H 22 May 2008*

HOE PROMENADE AND DRAKE

It's a view that, remarkably has changed very little in over 100 years, indeed it's changed very little since the replica of Boehm's Tavistock statue of Drake was unveiled here on Valentine's Day 1884 for by then the Esplanade, Elliot Terrace, the Grand Hotel had all been built. Of course the purpose-built Royal Western Yacht Club (itself completed in 1882), adjacent to the Grand, was destroyed during the war and was a bomb site for many years before the Azure development was built there. Furthermore the Grand has not operated as a hotel for a number of years now. There are other changes too - long gone too are the properties at the bottom end of Leigham Street - essentially, however, in a city that has seen so much change, the Hoe Promenade and the Hoe Park itself has been a wonderfully consistent feature of our landscape. *H 18 Jun 2009*

HOE BARRAGE BALLOON Boehm's striking statue of Drake - one of the few pieces of personalised statuary in the city - immediately catches the eye, as does Lorimer's magnificent Great War memorial, leaving us in no doubt that these two images are taken from exactly the same vantage point. The key to the number of years separating our Now image from the Then though, is the formidable balloon that floats on high above the Hoe. One of the many barrage balloons that were placed strategically around the city, it was held in place by cables that were designed to deter low-flying enemy bombers from homing in on their targets during the Second World War. Interestingly enough, one of the cables tethering this particular balloon, broke free at one point and the shackle at the end of the cable struck the mine at the top of the memorial, leaving a dent that is visible to this day. Note also the current retro-style lamp-post harks back to a different era than the one in our Then image, meanwhile the most conspicuous difference between the two images is the 1970 Holiday Inn on the left. *25 Oct 2009*

HOE MEMORIALS

Oddly enough, from this angle, the Naval War Memorial looks little changed, as the giant marquee erected for the University of Plymouth's September graduation services obscures much of the Second World War extension to Sir Robert Stodart Lorimer's original design (which is, incidentally, one of three identical memorials – the other two being in Portsmouth and Chatham). The Armada tri-centenary memorial on the other hand, does look exactly the same as it did when first unveiled in 1888. The town behind the Hoe Park however has changed enormously, not only in the process of growing and becoming a city but also on account of the bombing endured during the Second World War which necessitated major rebuilding and, in the case of two of the most prominent features in our early twentieth century Then image, St Andrew's Church and the Guildhall (now obscured by the Holiday Inn), reconstruction. *24 Oct 2009*

PLYMOUTH MARINE BIOLOGICAL ASSOCIATION

It all looks so familiar, not altogether surprisingly either for this view has changed little, in many respects, in 120 years, and yet wind the clock back just a few more years than that and this view would have been quite different and certainly quite difficult to achieve. Our Then picture was taken very soon after the new road in front of the Royal Citadel had been cut into the slope down to the sea (1888) and the Marine Biological Building had been (1887); and just three years after our vantage point had first been opened to the public. Having been superseded by Douglass's light in 1882, work straightway began on dismantling Smeaton's fine structure (which was found to be standing on a potentially insecure base) and on 24 September 1884 visitors were first able to enjoy this view. Subsequent alterations have seen the Royal Plymouth Corinthian Yacht Club constructed over and above the limestone outcrop beyond the bend in the road, less than ten years after this photo was taken, in the late 1890s, and the First World War, Royal Marine Memorial (1921). There are other changes clearly visible behind the Citadel wall and to the MBA itself, and of course many more besides in the distance. *H 19 Sept 2009*

PLYMOUTH MARINE BIOLOGICAL ASSOCIATION

For centuries the Royal Citadel upon the Hoe stood in comparative isolation: surrounded by ditches and ramparts, public access to the front of the fortification was not permitted until the Hoe was formally designated a public park, and a road was cut around to Fisher's Nose, in the 1880s. At same time agreement was secured to allow the Marine Biological Association to build their laboratory and research rooms here: it was the first such land-based building in England and put Plymouth at the forefront of Marine Science nationally and internationally, a position it still holds to this day, as this facility has been augmented by various other academic and research centres around the city, as well as the National Marine Aquarium at Coxside. Our Then photograph was taken soon after the original building opened on 30 June 1888 and apart from the limestone walls and walkways that were erected to support the new bathing facilities here in 1912, it is remarkable how little the area has changed - and while further development would spoil the character of the waterfront, the refinements to the Terrace restaurant are to be welcomed. *25 Oct 2009*

HOE BOWLING CLUB

Despite the tradition linking the Hoe with Drake's celebrated, pre-Armada game of bowls on 19 July 1588, Plymouth was slow to spawn formal bowling clubs. Indeed it wasn't until 6 May 1808, five years after the formation of the English Bowling Association, that a club was established here on the Hoe. Curiously enough, the first president of the English Bowling Association was the cricketing legend WG Grace. Back then interest in the sport had been revived nationally by celebrations surrounding the 300th anniversary of the Armada 1888, celebrations that included the unveiling of Gribble and May's Armada tercentenary memorial, far left, that same year. Our Then photograph was taken not long after the club opened, the First World War memorial being particularly conspicuous by it absence. *25 Oct 2009*

LOCKYER STREET

This early forties view of Lockyer Street shows the ruins of the erstwhile Hoe Grammar School (behind the Belisha beacon) and what was, at the time it was bombed, the Naval Nurses Hostel. Built as the Devon and Cornwall Female Orphanage ('Supported by Voluntary Subscriptions' as the wording below the eaves informs us), this was, as we can also read, established on XV May A.D. MDCCCXXXIV … 25 May 1884. Hoe Grammar had actually started in the street some 17 years earlier, in 1867, in No.6 Lockyer Street, later expanding into No.s 7 & 8, and part of Alfred Street. Sadly wartime bombing put an end to both premises, but it is noteworthy that their later replacements are sympathetic to the original lines and height of the earlier structures. It's also interesting to note that there are still two telephone kiosks on this corner, although one wonders how much longer they will be here. *H 09 Feb*

LOCKYER STREET

Instantly recognisable here our Lockyer Street Then picture takes us back to wartime, the best part of 70 years ago. The damaged properties you can see have long since been replaced by 'new developments' although I seem to recall it was still a building site more than 20 years after the war had ended. Those with longer memories may well also recall the gate erected for the King George V's Jubilee of 1935 at the Hoe end of Lockyer Street. Note the complete absence of cars back then and, consequently, the lack of yellow lines and street markings. Although, having said that it is likely that it was still too soon after the bombing and the little lamps in the street were doubtless there to dissuade night-time parkers from negotiating the rubble-strewn surface – after all the RAC sign on the left suggests that this was an area where parking was permitted.

LAMBHAY STREET

Our Then picture takes us back 50 years to when Lambhay Street as we see it here had just been built. Replacing a much earlier, cluttered but quaint collection of houses, courts and cottages, the new development at least made some attempt to maintain the street line and the original building heights. Remarkably the buildings look little different half a century on, the roofs have acquired a distinctive patina and there is a degree of planting now in evidence. Undoubtedly the major change, however, is in the vehicular department; not only are residents now far more likely to have cars, the street surface now needs to be marked out carefully and a line of slim black bollards are required to prevent inappropriate parking. Note, incidentally, the buildings immediately behind those in foreground had yet to be built and there was still a clear view through to the former Sutton High School on the far left. *H 09 Jun 2007*

CASTLE STREET

The street surface is fairly ancient and the vantage point is very much that of the first fort that ever protected Sutton Harbour - the one that gave us our civic badge with the four towers... although whether the supposed remnant to the left is the genuine article is somewhat in doubt. We are looking east from Lambhay Street, standing in that bit of walkway that runs under the late-fifties flats most of which enjoy this view. And what a changed view it is in the 30 years or so since our Then image was taken. Queen Anne Battery has been transformed from a largely working area into an almost exclusively leisure zone, with pontoons festooned with leisure craft, with and without sails. Behind the QAB complex it is yet more apparent how the working character of the waterfront has changed here, with few tanks left to store the oil and petroleum that conferred the name of Esso Wharf upon a part of the dockside. Note too the way the current health and safety guidelines have led to the installation of more impenetrable railings around the perimeter of Lambhay Street itself. *H 27 Jun 2009*

CASTLE STREET

Castle Street has been substantially redeveloped, many of the old buildings being replaced long before the war. But here as we head towards the narrow flight of steps that leads down to the Barbican, we find an element of the old world is still in place. Difficult to access by vehicle, a lone figure wheels a trolley up the cobbled street from the door of the Barbican Theatre, formerly the Seaman's Bethel. Note the narrow slit of daylight to the left of the woman standing in a similar position today - back then the steps leading down to the Barbican had a three storey building running across the top, adjoining the side of what was then the Brunswick Hotel. After the war the Trattoria Capri (later Buddy's Diner) would occupy the site of the   bombed hotel - more recently that has been replaced by the Mayflower Visitor Centre - now primarily a tourist information centre. *H 06 Jun 2009*

TEAT'S HILL

Our Then image takes us back a century or so, to a time when Teat's Hill and Teat's Hill Cottages were populated with boat builders, ship smiths, shipwrights, rope makers and fisherman, each trade an integral part of the working life of Sutton Harbour at that time. Today all of those buildings are long gone and although one or two were still with us in the 1980s, the area on the other side of West Pier was transformed, almost beyond recognition, after the lock gates were constructed and the National Marine Aquarium and the new Fish Market were built on substantially reclaimed land. The solid stonework of West Pier remains recognisable today, with 'The Prawn' the most conspicuous element of change on it's cobbled surface. Meanwhile on the water itself, personal pleasure craft of various shapes and sizes now dominate, although fishing boats still use the harbour in substantial numbers. *H 30 Aug 2008*

BARBICAN

The same place, but a different world - the Barbican 40 years ago. The fish market was in its prime with no thought of relocation, indeed the ice house, on the site now occupied by what was briefly a glass blowing house, was then a new facility, as were the offices either side of it. Although there's no date on the back of our Roy Westlake Then image, it must be post-1967 as close scrutiny reveals a likeness of Sir Francis Chichester on the former Crown and Anchor pub, which was renamed in honour of the solo-circumnavigator on the successful completion of his round-the-world epic in May of that year (the pub has since expanded into the adjacent premises and been renamed several times). Among the other notable changes we see there was still, Then, a bomb site in New Street (to the left of the Island House) and health and safety issues had yet to demand railings around the harbour walls, although there was a chain at least on this part of West Pier. *H 19 Apr 2008*

SOUTHSIDE STREET

For well over 200 years this quaint, late-eighteenth century, three-storey town house has looked out over Southside Street. In that time it has enjoyed a variety of tenants and neighbours - although Plymouth Gin, in front of which these snaps were taken, has kept it constant company throughout. W Woods – Dispensing Chemists, well-remembered for their bespoke jars of toothpaste, hair oil and other products – were here, for many years, prior to Jack Nash reworking this and its immediate neighbour, into the House That Jack Built, in the early 1980s. Similarly the old Coates and Co. bonded store to the left of Blackfriars Lane, and the Tope's building to the right, have both been refashioned as multi-unit properties with retail and food outlets. Looking remarkably similar overall, apart from the signage – even the Southside Street sign itself has changed – one element that has appeared since our Then picture and almost disappeared since, is Robert Lenkiewicz's controversial mural, now sadly faded after a couple of decades of exposure to the sun. *H 26 Apr 2008*

CIDER PRESS

There are few who would have predicted back in 1964 that this corner of Quay Road overlooking Sutton Harbour would become quite the fashionable quarter that it is today. Back then, in Peter Taylor's sixties snap we see broken windows on what is now the Cider Press (which opened as the Barbican Wine Lodge back in the summer of 1975) with Smokey Joe's (one of the Barbican's newer drinking holes) on the left. The narrow lane leading to Southside Street – and Stoke's Lane beyond it – is now home to several large wheelie bins, servicing these establishments, while Quay Road itself has been pedestrianised and divided up into seating areas to serve the large number of eating and drinking establishments that now line the waterfront – each one covered by a massive cream umbrella. H 28 Apr 2007

CUSTOMS HOUSE

It's hard now to believe but the local authorities pulled down more Tudor and Jacobean buildings after the war than the Luftwaffe destroyed during the conflict. More disturbing still is the fact that they achieved the same feat in the twenties and thirties and had it not been for protesting voices and the formation of the Plymouth Barbican Association in 1957, then all but a handful of old buildings would have been lost forever and the Barbican today would look like and late-fifties, early-sixties harbourside housing estate (viz the flats on the far left of our Now picture). Happily sense prevailed and the area has retained much of its historic feel, and is now home to over 200 listed buildings, among them David Laing's 1820 Custom House, which, to date, has enjoyed unbroken service as an Excise building - it replaced the earlier, sixteenth-century custom house, which still stands on the other side of the Parade. Happily what doesn't stand, and what, in fact, was never built, is the unsympathetic, two-storey community centre that was proposed for the Parade in the 1943 (post-war) Plan for Plymouth. *25 Oct 2009*

NOTTE STREET

One of the elements of surprise in the whole Then and Now process is stumbling upon unexpected differences and sometimes, unexpected similarities between images separated by the passage of time, in this case more than fifty years. 7 September 1955 is the date of our Then photograph: in it we see the corner of Notte Street and High Street (Buckwell Street as it now is) with Bill Ward's newsagents on the corner and a delivery bike propped nonchalantly up against the kerb – not a sight you'll readily see today. Difficult to get the exact same angle today as Notte Street is much busier than it was and even to get anything like the same view you have to stand in the middle of the road – indeed the road markings visible in our Now photo bear witness to the need to control traffic and prevent casual parking on this junction. Note too the loss of the quirky, decorative first-floor extension to the second of the oriel windows and the 'new-build' on the bomb site between these old corner properties and the Notte Inn – then the Plymouth Varnish and Colour Co. Ltd. *H 07 Mar 2009*

UNITARIAN CHURCH

When Roy Westlake stood outside the Then relatively new flats in Notte Street, there was very little planting between the buildings and the street line: now that planting is sufficiently mature to provide a complete green curtain during the summer season, completely obscuring the Then even newer property that was built to replace the Old George Street Baptist Church and the Unitarian Church just to the west of it. Curiously enough, although we can't see it in our current image, this is still one part of the city centre where roadside parking is still possible. *H 10 Mar 2007*

MERCHANT'S HOUSE

While it's not an unattractive piece of post-war architecture in itself the location of the Magistrates' ourt leaves a lot to be desired. St Andrew Street is one of the oldest streets in the city and it is a real shame that it has been neatly sliced in two with the construction of this building. While Mumford's premises (seen further up the road in this 1964 Peter Taylor pic) was a 1930s development, most of the rest of this street, which was little affected by the Blitz of Plymouth, was much much older, notably the so-called 'Merchant's House' from the beginning of the seventeenth century and the erstwhile Mechanic's Inn alongside it. Thankfully, and largely through the efforts of the late James Barber, the then Museum Curator, we still have the Merchant's House, a wonderful treasure in its own right which is full of fascinating bits and pieces of old Plymouth, including the old Park Pharmacy. *H 25 Jun 2007*

ARTS CENTRE

Concentrate on the cobbles and the basic topography of the street – the dip from the top section to the lower section: we're standing at the top of Looe Street, just a few yards from Plymouth Arts Centre. Since our Then photo was taken over 110 years ago, Looe Street has been widened in the wake of the demolition of all that you see on the left hand (northern) side of the street. The widening process occurred at the end of the nineteenth century when these Local Authority properties were built for local workmen. Fortunately for us the southern side survived that redevelopment; it also survived the air raids of the Second World War and the post-war Civic slum clearance scheme - thanks for which go almost entirely to the Plymouth Barbican Association. Formed after meetings in the Arts Centre more than 50 years ago, they acquired a portfolio of properties from the Council which they have subsequently put into good order and maintained: among them No.32 Looe Street where they set up the South West Image Bank and which is where we found our Then image. *H 30 May 2009*

LOOE STREET

One of the many properties that Sir Francis Drake owned locally, at one time or another, was here, near the bottom of Looe Street (the plaque at the top of the street is apparently in the wrong place). In Drake's day of course, this was very much at the heart of Plymouth. What we now mainly know as the Barbican was primarily an Elizabethan suburb of the town, a new area of development. Up until the late 1890s, just after our Then image (courtesy of the South West Image Bank) was taken, the street had changed remarkably little, but then, as part of an early 'slum' clearance scheme, the local authorities demolished half of the street, widened it and built Plymouth's first municipal housing. Some 50 years or so later a similar fate almost befell the other side of the street, however, thanks to the Plymouth Barbican Association, who were formed precisely to prevent such an occurrence, the south side was saved, and has been kept, largely by them, in excellent condition ever since. *H 16 May 2009*

28 LOOE STREET

Thanks Sylvia Blott of Southway for this quite quirky pairing. We are looking at No.28 Looe Street, two doors up from Looe Lane and just a few doors down from the Minerva. A grade II listed building thought to be essentially a nineteenth century townhouse with earlier elements, our Then photograph takes us back before the war, 'possibly to the 1920s', says Sylvia, whose aunt married the son of the woman in the photograph, 'at that time it belonged to the Flood family.' The lady's name was Elizabeth Flood and if we knew when she was born it might help, as the shop was in the Flood family some years prior to that – John Flood was recorded as 'shopkeeper' here in 1910.
Looking for commercial clues we find that Joseph Fry had been making chocolate since the late eighteenth century, so that ad doesn't help much, and Lyons had been in the tea business since the late nineteenth century, as had Robin starch, so those brands throw little light on the dating process. However, note how little the basic arrangement of doors and windows has changed in all that time. *H 17 Oct 2009*

CO-OP WAREHOUSE NORTH QUAY

A striking building that many thought should have been listed, the late-fifties Co-operative warehouse on North Quay stood, as it transpired, for little more than forty years. For a year or two the site remained empty but before long the present, eight-storey residential Discovery Wharf development had risen up on the site. The inevitability of such a move had already been heralded by the conversion of the much earlier warehouse alongside - now Harbourside Court. This early-nineteenth century structure was transformed from four stories to five courtesy of an interesting mansard roof. Predating the move away from warehousing was the early 1970s move in favour of moorings for leisure craft. Now there is little here to remind visitors of North Quay's industrial heritage, apart from old railway tracks still set in the cobbles, complete with one of the last examples of broad-gauge track still in it's original location. *H 06 Jun 2009*

NORTH QUAY SHELL PETROL STATION

Most people, when they think of a shell petrol station, will almost certainly think of a land-based drive-in facility frequented by cars vans and lorries, rather than the interesting curio snapped here by Peter Taylor. This was 'Plymouth's Refueller', the golden shell logo standing proud alongside the doorway housing a waiting petrol pump attendant. The re-fueller occupied a part of Sutton Harbour then very much home to working boats and working, blue-collar quayside premises and now packed out with luxury pleasure craft alongside professional, white-collar offices, upmarket accommodation and a few fashionable restaurants. Little then, survives of this view, save the quay on which everything is built, the water that reaches up to it and, a short distance this side of Hawker's Avenue, the converted former warehouse building visible on the far left. *H 26 Jan 2008*

KING'S HEAD

The nineteenth century facade offers little indication that this is one of Plymouth's oldest buildings and almost certainly the oldest building to have been in continuous service as a public house in the old part of Plymouth. Here for the best part of four hundred years (there is a piece of beam inside with the date 1629) the King's Head at Breton Side stands on the corner of one of the first mentioned streets in the town - Bilbury Street. Not surprisingly, however, there has been little obvious alteration to these two buildings over the last 50 years, the time elapsed between the images; the crenellations have gone from the pub facade - but all around there has been plenty of change, the towering Jury's Inn development behind, conferring even more charm on these, modest, three-storey properties. The faded giant Guinness ad on the earlier photo, incidentally, is a reminder that Guinness – and Bass – were both once bottled here. *H 08 Feb 2009*

THE REGENT INN

Apart from a few bits of cosmetic surgery and a name change (from the Regent to the Swallow) the focal point of these two images is much the same, notwithstanding the passage of time. In our Then image we see the then new office block which was built for the Transport and General Workers Union (TGWU) and the old Wesley Chapel better known to those that are still around to remember it as Selleck's Wesley Restaurant. Today of course the pub is framed in a very different way as new office, accommodation and hotel developments take the skyline to new heights in and around Exeter Street and now solicitors Woollcombe and Yonge occupy part of the former site of the Trade Union building, while the Union itself, locally, has moved into converted old premises on the waterfront. *H 28 Jul 2007*

RADNOR PLACE

It was back in 1920 that the Plymouth Co-operative established a dairy at Gilwell House off Radnor Place – a substantial operation that saw much coming and going over the years. At first, principally, it was a horse and cart affair, but increasingly lorries and vans took over, until transport and communications improved to such an extent that fresh milk could be sourced from further afield and the days of the in-town dairy here were numbered. Today Radnor Hall, major four-storey blocks of student accommodation for the University of Plymouth, occupies the site of the old dairy, while Regent Court, another residential development, dominates the aspect of Regent Street that we see here at the bottom of Radnor Place. *H 25 Apr 2009*

LANYON'S ALMSHOUSES

The original alms houses here on the corner of Green Street, were completed in 1680, only twenty-two years after Charles Church itself had been completed. At that time this view would have been very rural, there were green fields stretching eastwards across to Old Town Street and little or no development at all to the north until you got to Compton! Ebrington Street was more than a century away, but would be laid out by the time that the old houses, constructed with funds from John Lanyon's estate, were pulled down and replaced by these, more substantial properties in the late 1860s. Until the war Green Street was a pleasant little thoroughfare overlooking Charles Church graveyard, now these quaint houses overlook one of the busiest traffic junctions in the City – Charles Cross Roundabout. *H 13 Jun 2009*

BRETON SIDE BUS STATION

The Bus Station had not long been completed when Barry Trevethan took his snap sometime around 1958/9. It all seemed so clean and modern then. No need for crash barriers, speed humps and signs informing the public that the drop off point was further down the road and that this was a bus and coach only zone. I'm not sure there was overnight lorry parking available then either. Quite how much longer the bus station will remain here is unclear, already this scene has seen a couple of comings and goings on the highway above (first the disappearance of a large section of Ebrington Street and then the 1970s Drake Circus complex and car park) and the City Council have identified the site as one that needs to be looked at in terms of bringing the city and the historic precinct closer together and developers have expressed an interest in the area. *H 04 Aug 2007*

BRETONSIDE (*right*)

St Andrew's Church and the Guildhall had just been reconstructed, the Bus Station and the Bank were shiny and new as we turn the clocks back almost 50 years with this atmospheric shot from Barry Trevethan. Coaches are a little more comfortable and slightly more luxurious perhaps than they were Then, but the design hasn't changed all that much. There are however more double-decker coaches around and fewer double-decker buses as we move into the twenty-first century ... and there are no advertisements for cigarettes on the sides of buses these days and certainly no smoking on them or in the bus station waiting rooms! Note also one or two cars sneaking into the bus station to pick up or drop off coach travellers. *H 11 Aug 2007*

BRETON SIDE

Barry Trevethan, who took our Then picture has not lived in Plymouth for some 45 years, although he has been back from time to time. Anyone else, in a similar situation, who hasn't been back however, may be blissfully unaware of the fact that in the intervening years buildings have come and gone, on both sides of Charles Church: the infamous and unfinished Drake Circus car park to our left, recently replaced by the new Drake Circus Shopping Precinct, and Turnbull's two storey garage development to our right (only the circular inspection bay remains). In the meantime the then newly-built Bretonside bus station survives (but for how much longer), but the middle stretch of Ebrington Street has long-since been redeveloped, again with the area just to the north of it being redeveloped twice. Over and above these major changes, note how much more traffic there is on the road today; how many more buses (as opposed to coaches) used the bus station and how the slopes to the south of Charles Church have been refashioned. *H 14 Jul 2007*

CHARLES CHURCH

Our early image appears to have been taken from an upstairs window of a property in the now long-gone Vennel Street, which along with Norley Street and Green Street, formerly constituted the boundaries of the seventeenth-century Charles Church and its burial ground. Today only a part of Green Street survives (in the shape of the old alms houses on the eastern edge of Charles Church roundabout). In order to obtain a similar view today we have to take the moving escalator to the first floor of the Gala Bingo premises alongside Staples in the much criticized newish block on the southern side of the roundabout.
H 02 Dec 2006

DRAKE CIRCUS CAR PARK

There's something about the 'old' Drake Circus car park, which, from this angle, somehow reminds me of that popular, early, computer-based Space Invaders pub machine game. It's not especially pretty, but I'm reliably informed that it would have been much more visually-attractive had budgetary restrictions not stopped the concrete skeleton being faced the way the architects originally envisioned (the car park itself was supposed to be two storeys taller too). Notwithstanding all that, is there really anyone out there who would still prefer to see the car park and not the angled orange wafers and glass frontage which from here nicely reflects the tower of the seventeenth century Charles Church? *H 17 Mar 2007*

DRAKE CIRCUS CAR PARK

You sometimes wonder when architects and engineers plan buildings, whether they walk all around them in their mind's eye before they get them built, or whether it sometimes comes as a genuine surprise to see this angle and that angle, in a way they never quite anticipated. Certainly, while there can be no doubt that neither of these structures were designed to front this short stretch of Exeter Street above Breton Side bus station, we certainly don't see either of them at their most flatteringly photogenic. The erstwhile car park looks exactly the skeletal, unfinished thing it always was, while the bottom end of the new Drake Circus really does look like a bottom end – it's a bit like holding a camera to your backside nevertheless hoping that people will know you're smiling. A contender for the greatest ratio of wall to window (along with the grain silo at Millbay) in the city, it oozes a depressing dullness, broken only by that thin strip of window and a couple of business logos. *H 14 Apr 2007*

NORWICH UNION BUILDING

Completed and opened in 1951, here we see the Norwich Union Building, at the top of Royal Parade, approaching the final stages of construction. St Andrew's Cross roundabout is not that busy, which, presumably, is the reason that the middle of the roundabout is fenced off - to stop people taking short cuts right across the middle of the roundabout. Today, of course, that would be a somewhat perilous course of action, which, presumably, is the reason that the middle of the roundabout is no longer fenced off, despite the attraction of the fountain that now sets this area off. Meanwhile the lone bus entering Old Town Street, is a reminder of how this used to be one of the major through roads in the city centre - the late-nineteenth century Drake Circus was still standing then, with traffic meandering down past it on the northern route out of town. To the west of the building here, facing Royal Parade, the Pophams building, now occupied by Lloyds Bank, had yet to be built, but there was not long to wait. Within a couple of years the whole of the north side of Royal Parade would be completed. *Nov 2009*

OLD TOWN STREET

When Roy Westlake took the older of the two pictures here, this was very much a part of the face of the new City Centre. Back Then, some of these businesses were newer to the area than others; Thomas Cook & Son, 'the world travel service' had previously been based down at Millbay Docks, however today, some 50 years on, they're the only ones still to be found in this little stretch. The London Boot Company has moved on, as have Kendal & Sons the rainwear and umbrella specialists, and the Norwich-based Norvic Footfitters, a business that was established in Norfolk at the end of the nineteenth century and called it a day over thirty years ago. Alongside them, some will doubtless recall the pre-war Old Town Street premises of AR and HV Jeffery, where many a Plymothian got their first football boots, cricket bat or tennis racket. The post-war incarnation was here for many years. Underneath the awnings and a little further along we had Lockwood and Bradley, the drapers and Hepworths the tailors, with the familiar logo of Boots the Chemists on the opposite corner, above the Spooners' van. Now the café culture dominates this section of the partly pedestrianised street and one can only wonder what it will all be like in another 50 years. *H 23 Apr 2007*

OLD TOWN STREET

It's not quite possible to line these images up exactly but our rough guide is the eastern end of St Andrew's Church, visible, although by no means clearly, in both pictures, just beyond the block of buildings on our right.

Seventy three years - and the Second World War - separate the two shots as our Then image takes us back to Old Town Street as it was in October 1935. Of all the reconstructed city centre streets this is the one that most faithfully adheres to the original line, although, since the opening of the new Drake Circus a couple of years ago, the similarity between the two has been considerable compromised. Note the difference in the width of the pavements, and the contemporary situation whereby taxis have replaced buses and trams … in this area at least. *H22 Nov 2008*

OLD TOWN STREET

Looking down Old Town Street today it's hard for most of us to believe that standing in the same place some 70 years earlier this is the view that would have presented itself to you, and yet it is just possible that the schoolboy walking towards our pre-war cameraman is still with us to tell the tale, along with many others of a similar or slightly older vintage. Snapped sometime around 1937, note the absence of the Guinness Clock on the late-Victorian Drake Circus building - it would not appear for another year or so - and note the tram lines running down the middle of the road. There were no kerbside stops for the tram - to get on and off you had to step out into and across the traffic! *H 27 Dec 2008*

CENTRAL METHODIST HALL

Much the same but very different, that's the first impression when comparing these two shots of Central Methodist Hall. Separated by the best part of 50 years, our Then photo was taken on 22 August 1960, when most of post war Cornwall Street had been laid out but before the side extension to Central Hall had been built to front onto the new thoroughfare. Substantially added to in the late-sixties - the new hall was opened in May 1970 - Central Methodist had been earlier redeveloped in 1939. The earliest fabric of the building dates back to 1817. The thirties makeover was completed with money and encouragement from Lord Rank, the cinema mogul and keen Methodist who felt that new medium of film could be used to promote Methodism. As it transpired the war intervened and films weren't shown here, but the building did survive the conflict intact and for a time the bombed-out City Council held their meetings here. Post-pedestrianisation and post-redevelopment of Drake Circus there have clearly been further changes, who knows what this view will look like in another 50 years? *H 12 Feb 2009*

DRAKE CIRCUS

Our Then and Now images here are both taken from Drake Circus, only it wasn't quite possible to get the same angle and elevation as we are talking about two completely different Drake Circuses. The first was newly opened at the dawn of the 1970s when Roy Westlake ventured into the upper floors of what were then the Westlake stockbroker's office block, while the second was opened just a few years before Ben Robinson roamed around the new Drake Circus car park looking for a similar vantage point. In the meantime, the 1970s Drake Circus had performed over 30 years of service; been razed to the ground and replaced, since when the ground-breaking University arts block has appeared on the scene, dominating the foreground. *25 Oct 2009*

PLYMOUTH UNIVERSITY

The eight storey block of the former Technical College was opened in 1967. As of 1 January 1970 the college was officially restyled Plymouth Polytechnic and 22 years after that, it was once again reconstituted, this time as, what it had been in all but name for some years, the University of Plymouth. Throughout that time it had grown substantially, year on year, but the period of growth that followed the re-designation as a University was even more spectacular. The great driver behind much of that growth was the Vice-Chancellor at the time, Professor Roland Levinsky. Of all the new buildings he oversaw however none were more eye catching that Henning Larsen-designed stone, glass and copper construction that sits just south of the old main block. Sadly Levinsky was struck down and killed by an electricity cable, while out walking, sometime before the building - which was subsequently named in his honour - was completed in 2007. *25 Oct 2009*

GIBBON STREET

Right in the heart of student-ville, at the top of Gibbon Street, we find the Fresher and Professor. Formerly a modest beerhouse – the Grand Duchess, named after Marie, the Grand Duchess of Oldenberg who was a regular visitor to Devon - this has long-since been expanded into the two adjacent premises. The first of which was, when our Then photograph was taken more than 50 years ago, home to FG (Frederick George) Bassett's hairdressing business – note the familiar red and white striped pole that barbers typically used to indicate their trade. There were a few more businesses here in Gibbon Lane which runs at right angles to Gibbon Street, among them Mumford and Son's local pickle factory, the entrance to which can just be seen behind the woman rounding the street corner. Today the area has a more casual feel, typified by the cars 'artistically' placed on what was the first floor of the corner property. *Nov 2009*

WIMPY

Long a feature of Plymouth's post war city centre, the well-loved Magnet was, for a certain generation, one of the first restaurants they ever went to; with its red-brick walls and mock-Georgian window, it was a little different to the slab-finished Portland stone facades of it neighbours. But nothing lasts forever and as the eighties dawned the fast food chain Wimpy took over what had been very much a local treasure. Created by Eddie Gold, from Chicago, in the thirties (the named was inspired by the Popeye cartoon character J Wellington Wimpy), the Wimpy brand was licensed by Lyons in this country in the fifties.

In 1977 Wimpy became part of the United Biscuits portfolio, then Grand Metropolitan in 1989. Grand Metropolitan had bought the Burger King chain the previous year and this Plymouth outlet soon became a Burger King. Now the property is experiencing yet another makeover. Note too the changes that have befallen the neighbouring properties and the parking/pedestrianisation. *H 17 Feb 2007*

ST ANDREW'S BURIAL GROUND

Our Then image takes us back to before 1895, for that was when the burial ground here, north of St Andrew's Church, was levelled to create an open space and allow an easier tram route from Old Town Street into Basket Street. To mark the change, and honour the disturbed graves, St Andrew's Cross was erected on part of the site. The view offered here looks out across the bottom of Old Town Street (No.107 was County Co-operative Drug Company) and down into Whimple Street – to the left of what is now Café Rouge. The latter building, seen here on the corner of Whimple Street and St Andrew Street, had been erected as Plymouth's first purpose-built Post Office in 1848, and was then serving as the Western Counties & South Wales Telephone Company base – which doubtless accounts for the aerials on the roof of the building (note this predates the appearance of the statue of King Alfred – the motif of the Wessex Insurance Company). *H 18 Apr 2009*

ST ANDREW'S CHRISTMAS

Trying to take a photograph in the dark and find the right location, particularly when you are very near to busy traffic, is not the easiest thing to do, however, here separated by over 40 years, are two images of St Andrew's Church at Christmas. In the earlier version the Civic Centre had barely been up for a couple of years, and yet it looks little changed today, however, in the light of recent statements from the City Council about the building, one doubts very much whether it will still be there in another 40 years. It is, of course, much more likely that the tower of St Andrew's will still be here though, having survived over 540 years already. While our Now view gives the impression that there is no nod in the direction of festive lighting here today, and certainly no giant Christmas tree, the trees that line Royal Parade, are decorated, and they are also much, much bigger than they were back in the early sixties. *H 23 Dec 2006*

ST ANDREW'S CROSS

Admittedly there's a major difference in the time of year that these two photographs were taken, one at the height of a wet and warm summer, the other in the depths of winter, but even so it is obvious just how far the post-war planting of trees along Royal Parade, and in the middle of St Andrew's Cross Roundabout, has come on. Half a century separates the images and yet the buildings on the north side of Royal Parade still have a pleasantly contemporary feel about them. Back then, on the south side, the Civic Centre had yet to be built, and indeed, further away in terms of time and distance, so too had the Theatre Royal. But overall there have been remarkably few material changes to this grand and impressive thoroughfare. Incidentally, I wonder what that policeman was thinking!
H 18 Aug 2007

ST ANDREW'S CROSS ROUNDABOUT

So very familiar in its day and so very different now, here we are at the bottom of Old Town Street, with no hint of lasting reminders of the old Old Town Street, or indeed Bedford Street or Basket Street, which, from this position, some 70 years ago, lay either side of the Bateman Optical building. All of this is long gone, along with the original St Andrew's Cross and the Municipal Building, the architectural partner of the Guildhall. Our elevated vantage point today is the balcony of the architectural wonder that is the bank building at the eastern end of what is now Royal Parade, which in turn was laid out in 1947, a decade or so after our Then image was taken. Royal Parade had pretty much achieved its present look by 1962 with the completion of the Civic Centre tower block. Since then, the major changes evident in Graham Hobbins's Now photo have been cosmetic and horticultural. *H 28 Jun 2008*

BEDFORD STREET

The match of angles is necessarily approximate and anyway very difficult as although only 70 years or so separates these two images of Plymouth City Centre, there is no common reference point to fix upon. The Municipal Building on the left, survived the war, albeit as a shell, but was a foot or two in line with the proposed Royal Parade and so was taken down. The Prudential building at the western end of Bedford Street (with a cone surmounting its tower too) survived in a much healthier state, but its retention was never likely once the Plan for Plymouth had been adopted. Apart from those structures little else from our Then image survived save one or two other facades and one or two buildings (which we can't see properly anyway) in Westwell Street – running parallel to and behind Bateman's opticians. Curiously enough one link between the two images, although again they don't quite match up, is that the buildings we see on the far right of each image are both located on the south-western corner of Old Town Street, the modern thoroughfare running on similar, but not identical, lines to its pre-war counterpart. *H 09 Aug 2008*

MUNICIPAL BUILDING

The pillars provide the link between these two very different images. The curious thing is, however, that around the turn of the nineteenth/twentieth century (when our Then view was taken by William Gilhen) aspects of this view were very much a novelty, after all it had only been a few years earlier that St Andrew's Cross had been erected on this newly levelled area. Prior to 1895 the northern side of St Andrew's Church had been dominated by a large burial ground and a wall, surmounted by railings, which stood several feet higher than what we see here; inside the railings, hedges and other planting effectively screen most of the view of the lower part of the Municipal Building and the Bedford Hotel (later more familiar as Bateman's opticians) and totally obscured the view of Basket Street between the two. Today, of course, all that is long gone anyway and were it not for the pillars and the survival of St Andrew's it would very difficult to place the Then view. Incidentally it's interesting to note that the more elaborate of the two pillars was originally further around the perimeter of the burial ground and replaced an earlier 'plain' pillar. *H 11 Apr 2009*

ST ANDREW'S CROSS

As Plymouth expanded and became busier as the nineteenth century progressed, so the area at the heart of the town became more and more congested and right in the middle of that congested area was the dead centre of the town – the burial ground of St Andrew's Church. A large foreboding space surrounded by a high wall and laid out at a height that was well above street level, it blocked views and access into the Guildhall Square, Old Town Street, Bedford Street and St Andrew's itself. Thus it was that the decision was taken to move the burial ground to Westwell Gardens, to level the area in front of St Andrew's and as a special memorial to those who had been interred there, to create a special monument – St Andrew's Cross. In the event it stood for almost 50 years, but was deemed to be unsafe after the bombing and although still managing to stand, was nevertheless pulled down. Back in the 1890s, when our Then image was taken, we had the Victorian Municipal Buildings and the relatively newly-built Post Office in the background. Today, for the time being at least, we have the post-war Municipal Offices in the background, a welcome green space in the foreground and the entrance to the church to our left – then as now. *H 21 Jul 2007*

CATHERINE STREET

Eighty-one years separates these two images, our Then picture takes us back to May 1926 and the General Strike, and an arrested striker is escorted through Catherine Street, where the Police Station was based before its move to Greenbank. The Station, at the back end of the Guildhall is to our left, and the base of St Andrew's Church tower, to the right. There were few private motor vehicles on the road back then, but that didn't mean there were always this many pedestrians. This was the fall out from the crowds that had gathered in Old Town Street where trams and buses driven by ex-drivers and strike breakers had caused consternation in an excitable gathering. In the distance, Then, we see part of Bedford Street, today, Royal Parade it is that runs at right angles behind the trees. *H 05 May 2007*

ROYAL PARADE

There's still no roof on St Andrew's Church, the future of the Guildhall is still undecided, the trees lining Royal Parade are barely more than saplings and the National Westminster Bank has yet to rise up from the ground. We are looking down the first great axis of post-war Plymouth at the beginning of the 1950s; Picken's Wine Vaults, on the northern side of Whimple Street, is still serving customers. Time, however, is running out for both the punters and the property, perhaps unfortunately, as another peripheral pre-war survivor which could have been spared … is not.
H 03 Mar 2007

ROYAL PARADE

Half a century on and the buildings still feel comfortably contemporary, although clearly from this angle mother nature has worked her magic and when in leaf the trees dominate the view. Fashions have changed dramatically and generally fewer clothes are worn – in every sense. There are fewer double-decker buses, not necessarily fewer buses, stopping at the bus stops, which are much better designed and artily crammed with advertising. Considerably more cars now run up and down Royal Parade - despite the best efforts to keep this principal thoroughfare pedestrian friendly. And while this side of the road is still relatively green and open, car parking and heavy footfall have taken their toll on the former flower beds. *H 13 Sep 2008*

ROYAL PARADE No precise date on our wonderful Then shot from the South West Image Bank, but judging from the thoroughly modern mini heading up towards the not-much-older National Provincial Bank at the top of Royal Parade, we look to have travelled back to 1961 or thereabouts. The Leyland bus, closest to camera on the right, would appear to be No.135 (TCO 535) which entered the Plymouth service in the summer of 1960, and doubtless there are many readers who can readily identify and date the cars heading towards our vantage point: the 1957 MG Magnette, the 1959 Ford Zephyr and the two Austins A55 (or 60) and the A35 behind it – all of them British made, incidentally, and coincidentally, the front three at least, all sporting familiar, yellow and silver, metal AA badges. Among the changes that leap out most, note the flower beds, the maturing trees, the speed camera signs and considerably fewer double-deckers. *H 20 Sep 2008*

ABC AND DERRY'S CROSS Road to Perdition and My Big Fat Greek Wedding were showing at the ABC or MGM or Reel as it now is, when the late Ron Garratt took this photo of the building site that had, not long beforehand, been home to a petrol station and a large, open, two-storey car park. The cinema itself is the true survivor of this group to date, as both the Athenaeum and the old Westward TV buildings date from the dawn of the 1960s while the ABC, or Royal Cinema as it was when built, was opened the year before war broke out, in 1938: it stands on the site of the old Theatre Royal which was pulled down in 1937. Today the Travelodge occupies the car park site, with various bars and restaurants – Bella Italia, La Tasca, Varsity and Revolution – occupying the ground floor units overlooking Derry's Cross Roundabout. With various plans and proposals for the old TV Studios and the Roundabout itself currently on the table, who knows exactly what this view will look like in another six years time. *H 04 Aug 2007*

CO-OPERATIVE HOUSE

The first phase of what would come to be called Co-operative House (that bit facing squarely on to Royal Parade) was opened in 1953, the final, fourth, phase (fronting New George Street) would be completed eight years later, by which time the Co-op were occupying the largest amount of retail space of any of the post-war traders in the city. Not that the situation had been any different before the war, as the Co-op's impressive Central Premises had towered above most of its neighbours since its construction in the 1890s. Re-styled Derry's Department Store in 1998, in 2009 agreement was reached to sell the Co-op's interest here to the Liverpool-based Vergo Retail. The Plymouth and South West Co-operative still retained over 100 other retail outlets in the area. However a few months later another major decision in the history of the local Co-operative Society saw them agree to merge their interests with that of the national Co-operative Wholesale Society. Most of 138,000 or so members will not notice any difference in service or 'divi'. Throughout these changes Derry's Cross Roundabout here has bloomed but remains one of the largest, inaccessible, green spaces in the City. *Nov 2009*

DERRY'S CLOCK

Looking down Lockyer Street we see the Theatre Royal Hotel on one side and the Lockyer Hotel on the other. The former was built as a result of an initiative taken by the Mayor, Edmund Lockyer, and his Corporation, who wanted Plymouth to have its own purpose-built theatre at the beginning of the nineteenth century; while the latter was built some years later as Harvey's Hotel, later adopting the name of the street, to become the Lockyer (commemorating the aforementioned mayor) Hotel. Today, of course, the car park for the new (1982) Theatre Royal occupies the site of the Royal Hotel, which was bombed during the war, while the Lockyer itself and the little newsagents alongside it were the victims of redevelopment in the early 1980s. As for the landscape behind the clock tower, the buildings on the east side of Bank of England place were gutted during the Blitz while those on the western side survived through to the mid-late fifties. *H 15 Nov 2008*

THE BANK

The Lockyer Tavern, remember it? It wasn't built as a pub, but then neither was the building next to it, the Bank, which was actually built as … a bank. Nor was the Bank building as old as the Lockyer building, but, visually and structurally, it was more impressive. Thus it is that the Bank stands as one of the few pre-war survivors in and around the heart of the post-war city centre. It was sometime soon after the opening of the Theatre Royal in 1982 that the Lockyer came down, and that quaint little newsagents alongside it, after that it wasn't too long before the large greenhouse style extension was added on the back of the Bank and our mystery Then and Now photo donor, took a second snap. A generation later and see how the trees – and the lamppost have grown, and how well the beer garden has matured. Perhaps it won't be too long before another snap is order, depending how long it takes for a new development to appear on the Civic Centre car park site!

H 24 Feb 2007

WESTWELL STREET

Clearly the Guildhall tower is an obvious link between these two images, but strangely enough, despite what you might at first think, it is not the only one. Long gone are the trams lines, the tram wires, the old Post Office and all the other buildings seen here in our early 1920s view looking down Westwell Street, but still with us, remarkably, are the trees that grew in the old Westwell Street burial ground – they are the very trees we see in the Guildhall Square today, outside the Civic Centre building and as such just manage to make an appearance, behind the more recent greenery, in our now image. Hard to imagine a horse and cart as part of an everyday street scene now, but it is all still within living memory! Note the old law courts behind the brewery cart, in roughly the same position as their modern counterpart.

H 13 Dec 2008

GUILDHALL SQUARE

It all seems so modern that it's hard to believe that it's now more than 60 years since Royal Parade was marked out and the beginnings of Armada Way were laid across it. As we look at our Then photograph with the old Prudential Building still standing to our left, a number of old Westwell Street properties backing on to our view on the right and various other wartime survivors littering the landscape around the metal framework that would soon be Dingles, one wonders what everyone then imagined the new Plymouth would look like. Curiously enough the Prudential Building was newer to the city in 1950 than Dingles is to us now. There can be no doubt, however that Dingles (or rather the House of Fraser) looks more a part of contemporary Plymouth than the earlier red-brick building would have done, it being very much a hangover of Victoriana. *h 23 Aug 2008*

DINGLES

Perhaps one of the most striking things about this image of the almost completed Dingles building in June 1951 is the pleasing aspect of its main eastern face - that section of the building that now overlooks the service yard. Sir John Burnet clearly did not just design a building just to face Royal Parade, Armada Way and New George Street, rather it was a four-faced edifice and one that was also constructed to butt onto buildings that would stand alongside each of its east-facing ends. For well over fifty years, of course, such a view has been impossible, thanks to the completion of Royal Parade ... and as the trees have grown so even the greater part of the southern elevation of Dingles (now House of Fraser as the new sign proclaims) has been obscured from this angle. There are also a lot more cars using the car park too! *H 19 Jul 2008*

PEARL ASSURANCE HOUSE

Fifty years on, Pearl Assurance House is still comparatively unspoilt and while there is still retail on the ground floor, the upper floors have changed dramatically inside. Today flats occupy the space which formerly housed various departments of the Inland Revenue and Customs and Excise and the Ministries of Supply, Labour and National Service, Pensions and National Insurance. The Ordnance Survey Office (Field Work) was also here, as was the Board of Trade (SW region) Office and Plymouth County Court Offices. Some moved out sooner than others but all are long gone now. There have been changes to the traffic flow too, both along Royal Parade and along Armada Way; the old phone boxes have disappeared, an underpass has been created and then filled back in and, most recently, one of Britain's biggest TV screens has appeared here - any idea what it might look like in another 50 years? *H 28 Feb 2009*

PEARL ASSURANCE

It's not so much what you see that's still with us in our Then photograph that is fascinating, as what's there and is now long gone. The Pearl Assurance building was nearing completion and, out of picture, to our right, Dingles was already completed, and thus we had the very cornerstones of Armada Way and yet Armada Way itself had yet to be properly lifted off the drawing board that was the Plan for Plymouth. Looking up that now clear boulevard towards North Cross we see a number of pre-war survivors, all of them just counting down the days before the demolition men moved in. Looking closer to the position of the cameraman, note also the position of the pedestrian crossing of Royal Parade here. It's not that far to the left of our current crossing point and observe too the difference in bus, car and street-light design 55 years on. *H 31 Mar 2007*

ARMADA WAY

5 August 1951 is the date on our Then image. Dingles had been open almost a year and Dolcis next door had also been completed, but there were few new neighbours in the post-war city centre. There were plenty of streetside traders lining the visible section of the new New George Street though, attracting good crowds in the process. Armada Way had been plotted by the surveyors but had yet to reveal itself in all its glory and little had been planted apart from grass. The Guildhall at this stage still had an uncertain future, but by the end of the decade the shell would be rebuilt. Fire would later necessitate a certain amount of restructuring for Dingles itself, leading to the construction of a sixth floor, but it wasn't fire that provided the excuse to add a fifth floor in the early sixties. Now re-branded the House of Fraser – note the discreet signs between the third and fourth floor - one wonders what the view will look like in another fifty years or so. *H 22 Jul 2008*

SUN DIAL

Looking up Armada Way some 45 years or so ago you can see how the potential existed to create an impressive, tree-lined boulevard from North Cross to Royal Parade at least, and potentially up to the war memorial on the Hoe. Back Then, around 1963, North Cross Roundabout had yet to be created and it's just possible to make out Reeds and Boolds on the north side of Cobourg Street, just to the right of the top end of York Street - all of it soon to be demolished. Further to the left we see the then recently completed tower block at North Road Station, which today, from this angle, stands to side of the Copthorne Hotel. While trees provide a pleasant green screen to most of this backdrop today its interesting to note that the once familiar red phone boxes, have, for the time being at least, been replaced by less stirring counterparts. Meanwhile proving that time doesn't exactly stand still, the nevertheless static Sun Dial dominates the view today. *H 21 Sep 2009*

PRUDENTIAL ASSURANCE

November 1955 is the date on our fascinating early view of the Prudential Assurance building, which means that plans had already been drawn up for the Civic Centre building, although it would still be a few years before ground work would begin and the best part of seven years before it would be completed. Pedestrianisation on the other hand was doubtless not even a distant dream, although strangely it has been with us now for over 20 years – as has the sundial. Meanwhile almost all of the shops have changed hands: the Prudential wording (but not the logo) has gone along with Alexandre, Modella Fashions and the Direct Raincoat Company. Moss Bros have moved to another part of town and the Fifty Shilling Tailors, one of the first companies to trade from here, clearly belonged to another era – after all when did you last buy a new suit for £2.50? *H 14 Mar 2009*

PRUDENTIAL ASSURANCE

So much has changed, and yet so little. It seems odd to see the fine Prudential Building from this angle without the Civic Centre towering behind it, but who knows maybe one day, if the authorities have their way, it may happen again, briefly at least, until some other massive development rises above it. Interestingly enough the Civic Centre isn't the only newcomer here, however, as the strange little kiosk building in the foreground bears witness; was it planned from the beginning? Certainly it was an odd space before, as we can see from Barry Trevethan's late fifties study. Note, incidentally, how the lamppost is still in the same location, only much higher today and no longer on the street corner as pedestrianisation and the removal of the motorcar has softened the streetscape. *H 29 Sep 2007*

MARTIN'S BANK

Doubtless there will be a number of older Plymothians who can remember Martin's Bank, indeed some may remember a world populated by a number of different banking institutions, inevitably, however, most have now been absorbed by little more than a handful of major players. Martin's were founded in the early eighteenth century and had around 600 branches nationwide by the time they eventually opened a branch in Plymouth (in George Street) in the mid-1930s. Operating from temporary accommodation in Westwell Street just after the war, they moved into these purpose built premises on the northern-western corner of Armada Way and Cornwall Street in the late-1950s. A decade later, in 1969, Martin's were taken over by Barclays, who still occupy most of this building today. However while the core business inside the building hasn't changed that much in principal, clearly the level of electronic bank card business has radically altered the way we use banks today. Meanwhile the changes outside the premises are equally radical as the cars have been stopped and all surfaces 'pedestrianised'. *H 25 Aug 2007*

VIRGIN

It was all so very new Then with little indication of just how clogged up these streets would become as more and more people could afford their own car and would then chose to use those cars to get them in and out of the city centre. Half a century separates these images and yet you would really need to be at least 25 years-old to really remember the pre-pedestrianised Plymouth. The junction of Cornwall Street and Armada Way has looked pretty much like this for 20 years now, although some may recall the mini Stonehenge, the circle of stones that originally followed the removal of vehicular traffic in 1987. Meanwhile up at the far end of the street those pre-war buildings we can just see in our Then picture have not only been replaced by a 1970s development, but that development itself has given way to our new 2006 Drake Circus – what will it all look like in another fifty years I wonder. *H22 Sep 2007*

CORNWALL STREET

FW Woolworth was the first big store to open in the post-war City Centre, in 1950, and before the decade was out almost all of Cornwall Street had been completed. Here however, we see it, in Barry Trevethan's late-50s study, sometime prior to the building and opening of the Pannier Market in September 1959. With so many shops not finished or ready for business it's not surprising that there are so few people around, but little could anyone have imagined just how this part of Plymouth would look 50 years down the line. Partial pedestrianisation, along with major planting and landscaping have softened the environment and today this area is one of many that helps give Plymouth's shopping centre such a distinctive environment. Note incidentally, the pre-war houses between Well Street and Tracey Street still standing behind the newly erected premises in Market Avenue. *H 15 Sep 2007*

NEW GEORGE STREET

With Woolworths on the way out and Littlewoods already gone, this section of New George Street continues to evolve. Long gone are the opportunities for parking here, swept away in the pedestrianisation scheme that transformed the city centre more than 20 years ago and some 20 years or so after Roy Westlake snapped this sixties shopping scene. Happily however, despite the many changing signs of the times, the basic configuration of the buildings on either side of the street remain the same, the hard, rectangular arrangement of retail premises long since softened with the planting that has appeared where the cars once had right of way. *H 20 Dec 2008*

NEW GEORGE STREET

A Bus drives past the top of the New George Street, a lone car is about to turn into Old Town Street, and the area looks deserted. The shops are probably closed - certainly they are all fairly new. Barry Trevethan's late Fifties shot takes us back to an era when a number of major department stores had food halls in the city centre (there's Spooner's - long part of the Debenham group - on the right; when did the 'Est. 1857' disappear?) Two doors up from that is the fondly-remembered Moons shop, where many younger Plymothians listened to the latest record releases prior to purchase. Today it's one of the many fast food outlets in the city centre, alongside one of the many mobile phone shops - another development that would have been almost unimaginable 50 years ago. Fernley Wallis, long a fixture on the corner, has also gone from here, as the relentless hand of change has ushered in quite radical alterations, most obviously in the wake of pedestrianisation 20 years ago. *H 01 Sep 2007*

WOOLWORTH'S

Fifty eight years and a lot of memories separate these two images as we see Woolworth's in New George Street on opening day and in closing week. The first big store to open in the city centre after the war, Woolworth's waited for some time to be joined by other new stores in post-war New George Street, although it was the good company of one or two other pre-war survivors; notably the Regent Cinema (then rechristened the Odeon) and Leicester Harmsworth House, both thirties buildings and the latter the then home of the Evening Herald and Western Morning News, and the vantage point from which our then photo was taken. Today the façade of that building remains and a similar vantage point can be found upstairs in Waterstones' bookshop, but book displays make it difficult to locate the right window. Consequently our Now vantage point is from a floor higher, but note how the entrance to Woolworth's clearly has shifted to the west since opening day. *H 03 Jan 2009*

NEW GEORGE STREET

Plymouth's pre-war city centre shops were scattered far and wide after being 'blitzed out' in 1941 and W Barratt, boot dealer, was one of many that relocated to Mutley Plain, while they waited to move back into Plymouth's post-war city centre. For most it was a good ten years or more before such a move was possible. Barratts had been in George Street, at No.65, before the war, then, sometime around 1951/2 they were able to move into No.62 New George Street, as the City Council did their best to provide like for like sites. True Form on the other hand appear to have been one of the many multiples that moved into Plymouth in the wake of reconstruction, generally at the expense of an older local business. Note how the premises on the other side of Barratts were still not finished and contrast how different the two views look in the wake of the 1987 pedestrianisation of the City Centre. *Nov 2009*

WOOLWORTH'S

Sometimes, although an image doesn't really tell you anything you didn't already know, it does somehow serve as graphic reminder of information that its all too easy to forget. For example, there are a generation of Plymothians who can remember the Woolworth store opening in New George Street, and then there's a generation who maybe weren't there at the time, but know that it was the first post-war city centre store to open back in 1950. However somehow the whole city centre seems quite modern and it's not until you see an image like this one that you realise that it almost belongs to another era, one where few people had motor cars and so parking in town was not an issue - there were no restrictions or parking meters What is more, many family men rode motors bikes, and motorbike and side-car combinations were a common sight on the streets. Today such sights would be worth a lot of points in your street scene I-Spy book and although it's difficult now to see much other than foliage from this vantage point, the only reason that there are no cars here is because there are too many cars on the road - if that makes sense which is why this area has been pedestrianised since 1987. *25 Oct 2009*

FRANKFORT GATE

From this angle it is quite possible that some find it easier to place Barry Trevethan's early 1960s Then image than the current one – even though, in so many respects little has changed here. It is, however, the little things that we notice. The trees are the same, but my how they've grown; the shops are much as they were but the occupants have changed, as have the facia boards – I'm not too sure I don't prefer the uniform facia with the different names in different fonts. The windows above street level have all been renewed and the brightly coloured panels have all been replaced by plain white panels. The paving patterns have been completely refashioned and the bollards have gone ... and seating areas have been pushed out into the open square itself. How long will it stay like this? Not long if the recent proposals to bring cars up into Frankfort Gate off Western Approach bear fruit. *H 08 Sep 2007*

FRANKFORT GATE

The summer sun beat down on the as yet unfinished Frankfort Gate, the familiar corrugated panels shielding what was then still a building site from the gaze of the passers by. The young trees had barely witnessed more than one winter while the old men sat and gazed out over the relatively traffic free Western Approach – no need for barriers then. It's 1959 and the redevelopment of the City Centre has almost reached its western extremity, but it still has some way to go to the north and to the east. Remarkably the final piece of that eastern picture was still a decade or so away, and yet already it has been demolished. How much longer, one wonders, will this western end hold out? And, if it goes, will the massive pedestrian footbridge disappear too? Note incidentally how spectacularly those trees have grown, and how little the shops, in appearance at least, have changed. *H 23 Jun 2007*

WESTERN APPROACH

It's always interesting to see how quickly we get used to changes. Here, in this Fred Guy shot from 1983, we look up Western Appproach, to what was the Cardiff Arms pub, with a large flat space, created by the removal of the old railway embankment and the bridge over King Street, the flats on the left being very new. Within a few years we had the now familiar Toys'R'Us (formerly Sainsbury's Homebase) building and the Western Approach car park, linked to Frankfort Gate via the pedestrian bridge over the dual carriageway. Even before those developments had taken place, Pilgrim Primary had been built behind the pub on the site of the old Oxford Street School and the pub itself had been rechristened 'The Townhouse'. *H 09 Jul 2005*

UNION STREET

The remarkable thing about this set of Then, Then and Now images is that while the usage of the buildings has changed greatly over the years, the external appearance of the stretch of buildings on the south side of the Union Street, between here and the Octagon, has not really altered all that much since they were erected almost 200 years ago.

The oldest of the three images takes us back to the late-nineteenth century, before the electrification of the tram system and before the gardens of the properties on the northern side of the street were built upon. However several of the buildings we see here are still standing, apart from two or three at this end, which were demolished so that Horace Andrew could build his silent movie Picture House here in 1911. In the event it stood for barely 20 years for in 1931 this became the site of Plymouth's first purpose -built cinema with synchronised sound - the Gaumont. Later still (in 1964) this became the Odeon Cinema and Majestic Ballroom, and then, within another 20 years, the cinema closed and the venue was run as a nightclub in a variety of guises: Oceans, Monroes, Oz, the Warehouse and latterly as the Millennium. However today the premises is closed and has been for a number of years. *25 Oct 2009*

UNION STREET

Thanks to John Curno for this pair of elevated Union Street shots. John, who was born in Union Street 60 years ago, took the Then image 40 years ago – with a Miranda Sensorex camera. Two weeks ago, armed with his current camera and permission to return, he revisited the scene and took our Now shot. The scene is both strikingly similar and yet remarkably different. The Drake cinema was barely ten years old when John took the first image, today the all-new building that occupies the same footprint – and uses the same ship, the Golden Hind – is barely five years old.

Meanwhile a more obvious change saw the removal, in the early seventies, of the railway lines and the bridge that conveyed trains into Millbay, and construction of the Pavilions entertainment complex to the south of the street, and the car park and retail units to the north, in the late eighties, early nineties. Note the pedestrian footbridge in much the same position as the old bridge.
Beyond that there are many discernible differences as we move along Union Street and beyond – particularly when we look around the Brickfields and the re-clad Devonport tower blocks. *H 17 Oct 2009*

DUKE OF CORNWALL HOTEL

Just looking at the building itself it's very difficult to highlight any major differences between what we see today and what was there some eighty years or so ago, when our Then photograph was taken. The cars are the principal giveaway, and yet one can imagine a film company being able to arrange similar vehicles and costumes if they wanted to recreate that scene. They might also need to get an old postbox, lamppost and perhaps refashion the entrance porch. Remarkable as it is that this building should have survived the war unscathed, there can be no denying that all around the hotel there have been many changes. Among them: Millbay Station, the reason the hotel was built in the first place, is long gone, as is the church, St James the Less, just out of sight behind the hotel, and in their place, we now have the Pavilions and St Andrew's School. *H 10 Jan 2009*

NEW CONTINENTAL

The cars and the signage are the main indications here of the passage of some three-score years and ten: back Then the name Albion still applied to the earlier, west wing of what became the Continental Hotel. The Albion element of the hotel complex is readily identifiable as the lower part of the building and was erected within 15 years or so of the opening (in 1849) of the erstwhile Millbay Station, which it stood alongside. The Continental 'extension' was added in the first decade of the twentieth century and it wasn't until the early 1930s that the name was used as an umbrella term to cover both buildings. Now, of course, the building has long since been regarded as 'one', and the original entrance, overlooking the station site, has been superseded by the eastern entrance of what, since the late seventies at least, has been known as the New Continental Hotel. *H 27 Jan 2009*

MILLBAY DOCKS

It looks so very different now, but Chichester House is one of two major skyline keys to these two images – in the middle, incomplete and with scaffolding around it in our Then image which dates from 40 years ago. To the left, clear in the Then scene but barely visible from this, slightly lower angle, today we see the Duke of Cornwall Hotel, or at least the little tower room at the western end. Other principal features in the middle distance include the shell of the old Ballard Institute this side of Chichester House, and the large modern block that is Ballard House, that covers the old site and more besides, today. Meanwhile on the waterfront itself the changes are even more radical, as this side of Millbay has largely ceased to have a dock-side role – long gone is Jewsons and the other working buildings around it. Perhaps, though, the most significant changes are yet to come, as this view will look vastly different again in just a few years time. *H 03 May 2008*

MILLBAY PARK

An older generation of Plymothians can still recall the time a First World War tank occupied the plinth just inside the entrance of Millbay Recreation Ground. The tank was a 'trophy' of the Great War and there were a number of such exhibits around the Three Towns. Devonport Park still has a captured Boer War 'pom-pom' gun mounted in a prominent position, and for many years there was a captured German field gun (sent from the Army Council) at the top of the playing field at Plymouth College – note there is also a similar gun here alongside the tank. The Recreation Ground here occupies the site of the former Millbay Barracks, which in turn superseded the old Mill Prison. The park was opened for public use, 'subject to Military Regulations' on 22 June 1911, as the plaque at the entrance proclaims, 'on the day of the Coronation of King George V and Queen Mary'. The plaque below this one is more recent (1997) and commemorates the gaol (Millbay Prison) 'where over 1,500 American sailors were held in captivity during the War for American Independence 1777-1783'. *H 11 Jun 2009*

MILLBAY FASTNET

Our Then picture takes us back more than 40 years to 1967 and the preparations for that year's Fastnet Race – in the event it was won by the then 29-year-old French journalist, photographer, artist and sailor, Christian Fevrier in his Tina "Esprit de Rueil". Today this corner of Millbay looks quite different - long-gone are the great dock-side gas cylinders - and, in Millbay Road itself, the Valletort Mills of Flour Millers, Spillers Ltd and Hosken, Trevithick, Polkinghorne and Co. and the old, imposing, headquarters of the Millbay Laundry, Cleaning and Dyeing Company. That long high wall at the back of the docks now hides a site or two about to be redeveloped, thereby ensuring that this scene will look very different again in the not too distant future. Back on the dockside, the cranes too have gone, as the role of the docks continues to evolve and now the area in front of that great wall has been given over to eight traffic lanes for vehicles awaiting departure on the Brittany Ferries *H 05 Apr 2008*

MILLBAY RACING YACHTS

Without the benefit of our Now picture it may be a struggle for some to place Roy Westlake's evocative Then image. We're looking down what is now the approach road to the Brittany Ferry terminal at Millbay, much of the former Great Western Docks has now been infilled and with it much of what presents itself in the view as it appeared here some 40 years ago. There are, however, a number of identifiable landmarks still; among them part of Stonehouse Barracks to the far right – seen above the young lady in the mini skirt; the gable-roofed warehouse to the left of the visible barrack buildings, and, to the right of the dockside crane, the church tower of St Paul's, Stonehouse ... still there but even more difficult to spot today. What was the occasion? Clearly a race of some kind for these yachts, two of which won the East Anglian Offshore Barnard Cup in their day – Andorran (1965) and Scootica (1972) - first and second left in the front. Interestingly enough the same trophy was won by Edward Heath in his Morning Cloud in 1969. Two years later Prime Minister Heath and Morning Cloud were here at Millbay having won the Admiral's Cup, which ended here. *H 29 Mar 2008*

MILLBAY SILO

I can't recall featuring a Then and Now pairing so close together in time but these Ken Hopkins shots are certainly worthy of inclusion, not only for the unusual angle on this once-familiar landmark, but also for the great perspective it gives us on the space the building formerly occupied. The late-thirties concrete monolith that was the grain silo had a working life of little more than 40 years and for the last twenty-five years of its life stood idle as a reminder of a bygone age and a challenge to developers. Sadly no viable solution was found and over the last few months the building slowly came down as a variety of machines capable of mass destruction, safely removed what for many had been a familiar friend and for others a significant blot on the landscape. One wonders what the same scene will look like in another year or so from now, as one by one new developments start appear around Millbay. *H 17 May 2008*

PEDRO'S

Some will remember Peter Zessimides' restaurant as the Octagon Restaurant, others will recall it as Pedro's; in more recent years various transformations have brought us to the point where one of the city's first post-war independent eateries has become one of 13,000 KFC outlets around the world (the Kentucky-based company reckons to serve eight million customers from over 100 countries every day). Meanwhile, back in this little part of Union Street, another change over the last 30-40 years has seen the Firestone Tyre Company become part of another major chain, Kwik Fit. Formed in Edinburgh in 1971 and following the take over of Speedy in France and Pit Stop in Germany, there are today over 500 Kwik Fit centres dotted around Europe. Next door to it here, we see that another licensed restaurant has become a fast food outlet as the Annex is now Dillan's. Note also the changes in pavement width, street furniture and parking arrangements. *H 07 Apr 2007*

Union Street and New Palace Theatre, Plymouth. E 18737

NEW PALACE THEATRE

The New Palace Theatre was much newer when our Then picture was taken than our current Theatre Royal is now. Captured during the golden era of the electric tram, Union Street was one of the busiest, and most fashionable thoroughfares in the Three Towns. The main places of entertainment were all here, music halls and picture houses – kinemas showing silent films with live piano accompaniment. Today the street is a shadow of its former self. Fortunately, thanks to the listing of the now sadly neglected Palace, much of the 'strip' east of this spot, still survives – behind our vantage point however, it is a different story and, but for a handful of pre-war buildings, everything is wider, newer … and less interesting. *H 24 May 2008*

SMEATON'S BRIDGE

It was in the summer of 1767 that John Smeaton first produced designs for a bridge running between 'Mr Croal's quay to the opposite shore'. Prior to that time a ferryman had pulled himself and his passengers from one side to the other using a rope strung between the two banks of creek. Smeaton had been a temporary resident of Stonehouse some years earlier (1756-59) engaged upon the construction of the lighthouse that would grace the Eddystone Reef for more than a century and currently sits upon the Hoe. By 1769 his bridge was in use, although it wasn't fully completed for another four years. Significantly widened over the years, Stonehouse Bridge no longer has tidal water moving to and fro beneath the road as the creek was fully infilled to the north in 1972. To the south, however, the water is still a significant feature, particularly for Princess Yachts who have built up one of the biggest businesses in the area on the east bank, on the site of the old Plymouth Brewery. *H 08 Mar 2008*

ROYAL WILLIAM YARD GATE

The entrance to one of the most impressive set of buildings, architecturally, anywhere in the South West, the Royal William Victualling Yard Gate is fully worthy of its position. Surmounted by one of Plymouth's rare bits of statuary this epic structure measures 62 ft tall and and leads into a 13-acre site, about half of which was land recovered from the sea, while much of the rest was the result of 'hewing away at solid rock' as one nineteenth-century commentator put it. Begun in 1826, during the reign of George IV, the original intention had been to name it in his honour, however he died in 1830 and the Victualling Yard, which was not completed until 1835, was named after his brother William. Having spent a lot of his younger naval days in the area William, - 'the sailor king' - was a popular choice locally and sculpture is reckoned to be a good likeness. Today the site, which cost £1.5 to develop nearly 200 years ago, enjoys a variety of uses with many of the buildings now converted for residential accommodation. *Nov 2009*

Devonport Guildhall.

DEVONPORT TOWN HALL

It's the classic view of classical Devonport and, remarkably, it hasn't altered all that much in nearly 200 years, surviving the amalgamation, the Blitz, cultural change, and the demolition of the fine original Ker Street houses and the Hindu-style chapel that occupied the site of Ker Street Infants' School until 1904 (the infants' school too is now long gone). The buildings were all designed by the classically inspired John Foulston in the early 1820s. Foulston, like many architects around Britain at that time, was fired up by the books produced by artists and architects completing grand tours of the Mediterranean and the Orient. The views they brought back influenced Foulston in the design of the Theatre Royal – the project that brought him to the area – and the Town Hall here (based on Parthenon temple in Athens): the column, created to commemorate the name change from Plymouth Dock to Devonport (based on Trajan's Column in Rome), and the Hindu-style chapel and the Egyptian-style Odd Fellows Hall – now the Ker Street Social Club. *H 12 Apr 2008*

MARLBOROUGH STREET

With the notable exceptions of Fore Street, Ker Street and parts of Albert Road, pre-war street scenes of Devonport tend to be a little thin on the ground, which makes it all the more remarkable that this shot of Marlborough Street not only survives to show us what it was like then, but that, actually, most of what we see here is still with us. Unlike so much of Devonport, which apart from a section of Fore Street, a part of Ker Street, bits of Albert Road, and a small chunk of Duke Street, was either flattened in the war or bull-dozed in the subsequent redevelopment. At the time the Then photograph was taken, incidentally, Devonport was still a separate town, the amalgamation of the Three Towns (Plymouth, Devonport and Stonehouse) coming in 1914. Note that the street did not altogether escape bomb damage, Mr Slee, the butcher, was a victim in his shop at the far end and what is here Goldman's naval outfitters premises was also hit. *25 Oct 2009*

ROYAL ALBERT HOSPITAL

Plans for the hospital were first made public in 1860 although work did not begin until March 1862, three months after Albert the Prince Consort, after whom the building was named, had died. The architect for the development was Alfred Norman and one of the wards was named after his wife. One of the principal reasons behind the project was to tackle the problem of sexually transmitted diseases, which were, at that time, of great concern within the Royal Navy. However, Naval physicians were reluctant to inspect the men, and the men were reluctant to be inspected, and so this hospital was largely designated a 'Lock' hospital, where women, suspected of being involved in prostitution, could be locked up and treated and only released when they had submitted to physical and moral correction! Before long however this was operating more conventionally as a hospital. In 1934 it was restyled the Prince of Wales Hospital, becoming the South Devon and East Cornwall Hospital, Devonport, in 1948 and the Devonport section of Plymouth General Hospital in 1963. This erstwhile prominent landmark at the top of Passage Hill was demolished in 1983, although the two towers were kept to be part of the new residential development. *25 Oct 2009*

TORPOINT FERRY Nationally there are less than twenty steam/diesel chain ferries the first few of which were all built locally (Plymouth, Turnchapel and Devonport) and they were all designed by a young, Devon-born waterways engineer, James Meadows Rendel. His patron initially was Lord Morley of Saltram, for whom he created a "flying bridge" across the Laira, linking Plymouth to the South Hams. Impelled across the water by an iron chain, Rendel's first "Flying Bridge" was susceptible to spring tides and bad weather and so, in 1822 Lord Morley commissioned the twenty-three year-old Rendel to consider the practicality of constructing a bridge across the Laira - it was built a few years later. Meanwhile a further flying/floating bridge, for Dartmouth, followed in 1831, then Saltash in 1832 and Torpoint in 1834. The last two, coming more than twenty-five years before the first railway crossing into Cornwall, represented a great advance in communications with that county, the lowest road crossing of the Tamar being ten to twenty miles north of Plymouth until as late as 1961. *Nov 2009*

TORPOINT FERRY Ironically, although the Torpoint Ferries of today are much bigger than their predecessors, there are doubtless times when the human traffic, even allowing for vehicle drivers, is much lighter than it used to be when few people had cars and there was much greater reliance on public transport. However, today's ferries are designed, liked their predecessors, for the times in which they operate and the current capacity of the latest fleet is over 70 cars, a far cry from the wooden vessels that were crossing here in the early eighteenth century, when the service first began and when wheeled transport was a rarity in this area, as the local roads simply weren't good enough. *Nov 2009*

ALBERT ROAD GATE

Time was when this lone antique structure stood at the side of an elegant portal leading into the 'finest and most extensive establishment of its kind in the kingdom' - Keyham Steamyard. Designed, in the middle of the nineteenth century, by William Scamp of the Admiralty Department of Works, there was, originally, one of these fine towers either side of the gate at the bottom of Navy Row. The trees on the far left here, incidentally, were on the fringes of Sparrow Park, a small green area on a site, which, formerly stretched away to the south. Since 1950 at least that site, and the land behind our vantage point (occupied by the erstwhile William Street) has been taken over by the Dockyard. In the early 1970s there was further change as the construction of massive, covered, three-hangared Frigate Complex spelt the end for this entrance, its replacement being a foreboding and desperately unattractive stretch of wall capped by a menacing stretch of barbed wire. *Nov 2009*

ALBERT ROAD

Known for many years in the first half of the nineteenth century, and earlier, as Navy Row, here, in this fascinating pair of period pieces we see Albert Road, Devonport. Some 75 years or more separates the two images, the delightful No.49 tram having been taken out of service in 1935 after 25 years of service. One of a batch of a dozen similar vehicles that was commissioned in 1915 No.49 was latterly very distinctive: most of its contemporaries were repainted in the Corporation's maroon and ivory livery between 1931 and 1933 while No.49 was given a 'one-off', chocolate and white, paint job. In those days of course, most people were heavily reliant on public transport, now it is mainly the older generation or, as in our Now image, the younger generation. Note incidentally that while there have been great changes on the south side of Albert Road, the north side is still much the same. *Nov 2009*

HMS DRAKE

Any Then and Now comparison can generate an interesting game of 'spot the difference', but this is a particularly tricky one. Everything here seems to line up - well almost. The clock tower at the entrance here to the Naval Barracks provides the central key, with the cupola at the top of the Drake Wardroom clearly aligned in relation to the tower and the guardroom, and indeed the archway to the left of this entrance into the base, while to the far right here, even the phone box maintains a constant vigil. But what of the right side archway, it doesn't line up! Has our cameraman got it slightly wrong, or has the archway been moved? Clearly it has, in order that larger loads can come in by land to this imposing late Victorian naval establishment. *Nov 2009*

WOLSELEY ROAD Thanks to Ern Downey (aka Ernie Kenny) for this slightly quirky Then & Now. The Then image was taken by Ern in 1955 outside the house he was then living in, in Wolseley Road. The focal point of his composition was his pride and joy at the time, his Jawa 350cc twin-stroke motor-bike. However Ern points out that in the background is the old St Budeaux Baptist Chapel – 'the baptismal font and basement rooms are still there buried under tons of concrete.' They built a new chapel in Fletemoor Road in the early sixties. The site was then used as a car showroom/garage run by Chapman's garages. It was converted to its present state in the early seventies, although it no longer sells fuel, it is being run by some hard-working, enterprising young chaps as a hand carwash. The Now photo was taken from exactly the same spot. 'I had to wait until the leaves were gone off my mum's lilac tree. The view hasn't changed much, except where there was a corner shop there is now a KFC and there were quite a few private houses in that part of Wolseley Road. At the time the first photo was taken the Southern Railway used to run next to the road, opposite our house – when a train went past you could feel the house shake.' *H 17 Jan 2009*

ST LEVAN ROAD VIADUCT

On the face of it there may not appear to have been that many years separating these two images, however more than 20 have now passed since the St Levan Road, or Ford, Viaduct was demolished. Officially opened on 30 May 1890, the massive, seven-arched, construction which spanned a 135 yard stretch across St Levan valley, had not been used for almost 23 years when it was finally taken down in 1987 - the last train having called at Ford Station on 6 September 1964. Trains had been crossing the erstwhile inlet (Keyham Lake reached up to this point until the nineteenth century) since the building of Keyham Viaduct in the late 1850s, and will doubtless continue until transport enters another age – meanwhile notice how the street markings have changed in the last 20 years to reflect increasing road activity. *H 01 Dec 2007*

SALTASH FERRY

This wonderful set of Then Then and Now images graphically illustrates the changes that have been seen here over the last hundred years, set against a backdrop that has been remarkably constant over all that time.

Back at the beginning of the twentieth century the ferry here was something of a ramshackle affair wide enough to take a horse and cart or two but ill-equipped for the traffic that would come onto the roads over the next decade or so.

Fifty years ago, the ferry was a fondly remembered but not desperately convenient affair that ran from infront of the Ferry House Inn to a point just south of Brunel's Royal Albert Bridge on the Cornwall side of the Tamar.

Today, although you could be forgiven for thinking that the car on the slipway here was awaiting the arrival of the ferry, that service - which dated back to the early fourteenth century - no longer runs. Indeed the last crossing was late on the evening of 23 October 1961. It was succeeded, the following day by the long-awaited road crossing which was opened the following day, alongside the railway bridge. *Nov 2009*

TAMAR BRIDGE

Two dramatic images offering a fantastic perspective on these two crossing points over the Tamar. Brunel's masterpiece, the Royal Albert Bridge, celebrated its 150th anniversary this year (having been officially opened in May 1859) while work on the road bridge began 50 years ago, in July 1959. Here we see the work in the early stages, at that point at which you see why it's called a suspension bridge, because the road was to be suspended off the those great steel cables. When completed this was Britain's longest suspension bridge, while more recently, in 2001, it gained fame as the first suspension bridge in the world to be widened - note the slight kink at this end where the extra lane on this side goes out around the tower. *Nov 2009*

RIVERSIDE

At first glance you might be tempted to think that not a lot has changed here and that little time separates the two images, but in fact these two images were taken almost fifty years apart, the Now image in the late summer of 2009 and the Then sometime around 1960. Look carefully at the bottom of the Brunel Bridge, as it was and see how now there is an extra layer behind, it being the roadway of the Tamar Bridge, which at that time had not yet been put in place. Indeed while the great suspension cables are in place, work on them is far from finished and the tower on the Saltash side is also still under construction. All of which means that the Saltash Ferry was still running, its eastern destination being a point just to the left of our vantage point here at Saltash Passage, or Riverside, as some call it. There is another major difference too, note the massive increase in the number of pleasure craft moored in the Tamar - easy to count them back then, try doing it now! *Nov 2009*

SALTASH PASSAGE

When Edgar Lacey took this view of the little park area at Saltash Passage some fifty years ago, the unusual five fingered granite memorial honouring the Americans of the V and VII Corps was very new having been unveiled in May 1958: for these US units Normandy Way had been United States Army route 23, and this their point of departure in June 1944. It wasn't long after that the Brunel Bridge celebrated its centenary, in May 1959, and shortly after that, in July 1959, work commenced on the construction of the Tamar Road Bridge. The cranes working on the assembly of the eastern tower can be seen clearly beyond the park and many were they who came along with their cameras to record the ongoing work. Forty years later, work began on extending that bridge, meanwhile there had been a number of changes in the park itself: a park that is a wonderful vantage point to watch the world go by, and to watch the sun go down, whatever building work is or isn't going on around the place. *H 31 Oct 2009*

CHAUCER WAY SCHOOL

The road may look almost as quiet today, but closer inspection reveals many more cars dotted around the front of Chaucer Way Primary School at Honicknowle. More than 50 years separates these two images and while perhaps there are more similarities than differences today, this time next year it will be a very different story. By then Chaucer Way will have amalgamated with West Park Primary and this site will be well on the way to redevelopment, and this school, which opened here at the dawn of the 1950s will have disappeared forever, leaving several generations with little more than faded memories and old photos. *H 29 Nov 2008*

GOLDEN HIND

Although the Parkway, cutting a carriageway across the top of Plymouth, was planned when this was the top end of town, it wasn't built for 40 years by which time this had become virtually the geographic centre of the city. Before that, the late-thirties Golden Hind public house (one of the few pubs in Plymouth today to reference Sir Francis Drake in any way – the Golden Hind was the new name given to the ship in which he circumnavigated the world) had a large clear space in front of it – a wide pavement and generous parking provision. Today with the city's most complex flyover arrangement alongside it, that has all changed, the pub itself however has remained delightfully true to its original appearance and is one of just a handful of red-brick – most of them immediately pre-war - drinking establishments in the area. *H 19 May 2007*

PENNYCROSS PARK ROAD

It's August 1964, the Beatles have conquered the world and we're standing on the corner of Langstone Road (although formerly part known as Langstone Terrace) and Beauchamp Road looking across to the corner of Pennycross Park Road and Langstone Road. Cave's Pennycross Stores, with the big Baked Beans ad, is on the corner next to a local draper's shop - there is a hair and beauty place there now. Meanwhile also serving the community, back then, in Langstone Road, we had Marion's stylists alongside the local chemist - today Newberry and Payne, the soft furnishing specialists occupy the same premises. Back then we had the very substantial Plymouth Co-operative Society Bakery behind us, now that site is occupied by a Homebase unit. *H 04 April 2009*

STADIUM FISH BAR

Ham Drive, August 1961, Johnny Leyton was top of the pop charts and life was much the same and yet also very different; can you imagine anyone putting up an outside, wall-mounted cigarette machine today? But this was the age of the outdoor vending machine, note also the ZY chewing gum machine... remember   the jingle? "Buy some YZ Chewing Gum, Smashing you'll agree, with the fourth you'll get one more, an extra packet free" - a bonus packet on the fourth turn on the knob when the arrow pointed forwards. The fish bar itself was open twice daily (but not Mondays) 11.30am to 1.15pm and 8pm to 10.45pm - nothing for the early tea market then! Somehow the building looked more interesting then; it's so much starker now. Long gone is the Stadium itself, then regularly alive with the throb of the speedway bike and the smell of that special fuel, the roar of the stock car and the excited bark of the greyhound, all largely superseded by the hypnotic screens in the corner of every modern living room. *H 19 May 2007*

MONTPELIER SCHOOL

Looking out across Parker Road, from its junction with North Down Road, we see, notwithstanding the fact that our Then picture was taken in the winter and our Now picture in the summer, that the trees here have grown spectacularly in the 25 years that separates these two images. Montpelier School can still be seen quite clearly through the foliage but it certainly now enjoys a greater degree of seclusion at this time of year. In the foreground itself it is interesting to see that this corner has been fenced off and that today's lamp-post is not only in a slightly different position, but that it is also considerably taller than its predecessor. The distinctive concrete litter bin, incidentally, is still with us, hidden by the fence but alongside the 'children crossing' Patrol sign. *H 16 Aug 2008*

OUTLAND ROAD

The changes are subtle but there are plenty of them. A difference in the seasons clearly have an impact on the amount of foliage visible in our Then image, while the advances in technology have had an impact on the need for telegraph poles. However it is the introduction of the pedestrian footbridge over Outland Road, here, just outside Devonport High School for Girls, that has been the biggest element in the change process. We can only see the underside of it in our 'Now' image, but one obvious effect has been the moving of the bus stop to its current location. Otherwise we can see that the street lighting has been renewed but not fundamentally altered, and the street markings are a little more complicated than they were a generation ago when our Then picture was taken in the early 1980s. *H 17 Nov 2007*

CENTRAL PARK Central Park was opened on 29 July 1931. Work had begun on the amenity a year or two earlier when the mayor, James Churchward, had cut the first sod in a development that had first been proposed by local architect Arthur Southcombe-Parker at the end of the Great War. The project had still to be completed when first opened – part of the idea behind it all being that the work should be 'expedited to provide relief for unemployment in the city.' The 234-acre site was laid out to include two bowling greens, eight match-size, green, hard tennis courts, 144 acres of playing fields and 'a modern car park to accommodate over 1,000 cars' – quite a visionary move at a time when most were reliant on the public transport that came in and out of the Milehouse bus and tram depot just out of picture Then, as Now, to our right. Note how an acre or two of green has been eroded away here in the meantime however, to allow for improved traffic arrangements at this now very busy junction. *Nov 2009*

MILEHOUSE BUS DEPOT In October 1919 HP Stokes arrived in Plymouth as the new general manager of Plymouth Corporation Tramways. At that stage there were only trams serving the public transport needs. Permission had been granted to allow them to start operating buses but all the suitable chassis had been pressed into military duty during the great war. However Stokes now pressed for the use of buses and in the summer of 1920 twenty, primrose-yellow vehicles started work on four routes around the city. Soon dubbed 'yellow perils' or 'boneshakers' these unforgiving solid-tyred monsters were not instantly popular - it didn't help that two pedestrians were knocked down and killed in the first year of their operation. In 1922 the last stretch of Plymouth tramway was laid (along Alma Road) and the following year this impressive new P CT office was built. Two years later the pneumatic tyre arrived and the golden age of the tram had passed, although the last one ran through until 1945. *Nov 2009*

PEVERELL CO-OP

Opened as Jubilee Stores in 1910, the Jubilee that was being celebrated was not a royal one, rather it was the 50th Anniversary of the Plymouth Mutual and Industrial Co-operative Society Limited - the 'Cwop'.

When first erected this was an impressive development on the outskirts of town; the Peverell estate was well-underway - but by no means complete. The rapidly expanding population needed shops and facilities, and the Co-op had also recently built a massive bakery at Peverell.

Our Then image however doesn't take us quite as far back as that time, when trams trundled around this corner, rather this dates from the late 1960s just before this corner site was given a major makeover and the clover leaf Co-op logo made its first appearance.

Today that facia still survives and a popular Post Office operates in the corner unit.
Nov 2009

CO-OP PEVERELL PARK ROAD

In 1893 Peverell Park Road was nothing more than an unnamed footpath and there was little in the way of housing development extended beyond Hyde Park. Over the next few years, however, Plymouth re-drew its boundaries to include this part of Mutley; part of the Pounds Estate was sold to enable development and in 1903 the rapidly expanding Plymouth Co-operative established a new outpost here at the junction of Peverell and Weston Park Roads. Over the next few years Hyde Park Schools, St Gabriel's Church and Peverell Park Methodist appeared, trams started to clank down Peverell Park Road (note the overhead wires in the photo) and terrace after terrace of housing appeared, fully justifying the Co-op's decision to erect a substantial new premises here. Remarkably over 100 years on, the same organization is still trading here, although clearly much has changed in the way of buying and selling food. *H 02 May 2009*

BURLEIGH MANOR

In the late eighteenth century anyone finding themselves negotiating the ancient Burleigh Lane would have found an imposing manor house on the other side of the hedge. It was one of the few properties in the area and for the next 150 years or so there was little change here. Then, as the Peverell estate branched out to the south and west, in the early twentieth century and within another decade or two, the Tor estate appeared to the north and east, so the neighbourhood changed. Requisitioned by the Ministry of Labour and National Service at the start of the Second World War, the site was earmarked for educational purposes after the war and in the 1950s Burleigh Secondary Modern School was built here. It stood just less than 40 years and following its demolition in the summer of 1990 the Burleigh Manor estate was laid out in the old grounds of the house and school. *H 06 Oct 2007*

SEYMOUR ROAD

As the population of Plymouth expanded spectacularly through the nineteenth century, so those who could afford to get away from it all started to take advantage of the improved roads and transport and move out of town. After a number of substantial properties had been constructed off either side of North Hill, so the more adventurous moved out to the west side of Mutley Plain and the gracious villas around Ford Park appeared in the 1830s. Hyde Park Terrace appeared the following decade and gradually Townsend Hill was populated with large residences. Then, in the 1850s Messrs Ellery, Fowler, Bennett acquired the two fields known as the Mannameads from the Seymour Estate and started building a series of grand villas. Our Then photo was taken some years later but just before these gate posts were taken down (around 1897) to widen the entrance to the still relatively new estate. *H 09 May 2009*

BARTON BUILDING

It's one of the city's more distinctive and delightful art deco buildings and remarkably, at first glance, it looks almost as good today as it did when it was first opened, as a car showroom, almost 80 years ago. Unfortunately, the wonderful window arrangement has been compromised in recent years and modern signage has affected the overall integrity of the building. Opened in 1930, on the crest of a car sales wave, the Barton Building was the city's newest temple to the motor car, with Morris - and Austin and Wolseley - their main lines. Forty years later its windows full of 1100s, 1800s, and MG's the building was still operating as a car showroom, with its wonderful wooden floor, balustraded balcony, and garage underneath, with petrol outlet alongside. Today the building is split into various units, but the view across from the Hyde Park Hotel remains little changed. *H 06 Dec 2008*

MUTLEY METHODIST

Time was when every December would see a seemingly life-size nativity scene at the entrance to the erstwhile Mutley Methodist Church. The long familiar spire and ecclesiastical, limestone pile on the corner of Belgrave Road has been gone almost 30 years now and a modern brick-built structure stands in its place. A little closer to our vantage point, but still on the other side of the road, Lloyds Bank (since remodelled as Lloyds TSB) still occupies the same building, however the Millbay Laundry premises has become one of Mutley's many estate agents and the Widgers outlet next door has become an extension of Boots 'Dispensing Chemists' alongside it. A more radical transformation has seen the National Provincial Bank morph into the Mannamead public house. Meanwhile, whereas in the late-1970s it was still possible for pedestrians to amble freely across the busy thoroughfare, now a long metal barrier coerces walkers to cross at one or other of the many sets of lights that regulate the traffic flow along the Plain. *H 08 Dec 2007*

FORD PARK CORNER Signs of the times … if ever there was a Then and Now comparison where the words say it all – this is it. Our Then image takes us back to 1930 when Albert Pengelly's chain of Tobacnists – the misspelling, accidental at first was adopted as a trademark for business – were spread across the City and the South West. This, though, was the registered office, of an organisation specialising in selling cigarettes, cigars and tobacco in whatever form that was required, and while the Pengelly empire might have been the biggest locally, theirs were by no means the only tobacconists in town – there were the best part of a hundred dotted in and around Plymouth. Eighty years on and society has changed, as has Mutley Plain Specialist tobacconists have all but disappeared in a world that no longer encourages smoking and after a variety of uses the old Pengelly premises is now split between a house-sales and letting agency, an employment agency and a charity shop – and today there must be a hundred or so of them around town, many on Mutley Plain itself. *14 Nov 2009*

NORTH ROAD STATION

It's difficult to date our Then image here; clearly the most notable absentee from our Now picture is the signal box to the right which has gone in the last 20 years or so, while the lack of the Plymouth Station tower block suggests that we're winding the clock back a good 50 years … or more. There are doubtless many other clues – signals suggesting a more precise location in time - and I'm sure there will be a few railway buffs who will be able to supply an even better date on this apparently pre-war view of the station that was first opened at the eastern end of the area known as Five Fields in 1877. Meanwhile more careful observation shows the Cathedral and the tower of St Peter's puncturing the skyline in both images, while examination of the platform arrangement and the track layout suggests that there is a somewhat simpler traffic flow in and out of North Road today. H 15 Dec 2007

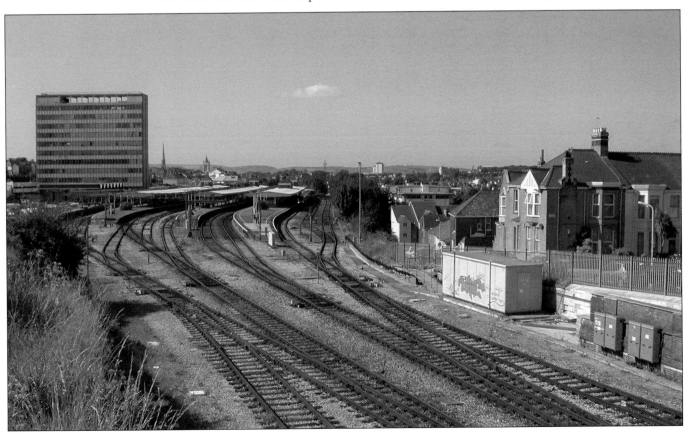

HEADLAND COLLEGE

Until being forced out by the Blitz in 1941, Mary Normington ran a private girls' school here on the corner of Headland Park and North Hill. With roots stretching back into late-Victorian times, Mrs Normington had taken the school on in 1906, and in 1941 she successfully relocated the institution to Gunnislake – rather like Mount House School at Hartley moved out to Tavistock. Unlike Mount House however, Headland College did not survive its principal. Mary Normington retired on medical grounds at the end of the summer term 1949, and unable to find a suitable alternative location, closed the school – she died six months later, at the age of 69. After the war Gard & Co, accountants, occupied what had become 1 & 2 Headland Park (1 & 3 before they were renumbered) and today the property is once again occupied by students, but students who have finished their schooldays.

NORTH HILL

The line between the bus bay and the main road surface marks the line of the old kerb here, and many will remember when the gardens of the houses to the left stretched further down to this old low wall - now removed. Back then the shops along here were busier than they are now, the footfall has reduced as more people get around by car and fewer people walk. Nevertheless the changes, from this perspective, appear relatively few considering that some 50 years have elapsed since our Then photograph was taken. The main alteration to the landscape is the new apartment block built by David Holmes in the last year or so, on what was one of the last city bomb sites, at the end of Headland Park. *H 31 Jan 2009*

PLYMOUTH HIGH SCHOOL It was in 1872 that a freehold site here adjacent to a Jacobean house known as North Hill, was acquired by the trustees of the South Devon and Cornwall Institution for the Blind. Shortly afterwards the governors of the newly constituted Devon and Cornwall Girls' School Company purchased the site behind it for £3,000. In the event the Blind Institution opened here in 1876 and Plymouth High School for Girls the following year. At the dawn of the 1890s a south wing was added to the Blind Institution, partly obscuring the view of the school from the road, nevertheless for almost ninety years the two operated side by side. The south wing was rebuilt after being bombed during the war, but in 1964 the Blind Institute moved to Stonehouse and Plymouth High subsequently annexed the whole site. Note the lady in the 100-year-old Then picture carrying two wicker shopping baskets that were typical of the sort of work then produced in the Blind Institute. *H 02 Feb 2008*

FIRE STATION

Anyone who has been away from Plymouth for the last ten years or so will doubtless marvel at the changes, not just around the city centre and Sutton Harbour, but in various other locations around town, notably here in the area, chosen by our Victorian forebears for Plymouth's Prison, Workhouse and first major hospital – Greenbank. In the 1920s some of the workhouse buildings were adapted for another hospital – Freedom Fields – and then, in 1936, Greenbank Fire Station was built on part of the site of the old prison. That same year the Police Station moved into another part of the prison buildings. Today only the Fire Station remains, and that, as you can see, has been rebuilt in the last ten years, meanwhile the two hospital sites have been redeveloped for housing and the rest of the prison site will soon follow suit. *H 30 Jun 2007*

ALEXANDRA ROAD

This corner has long been one of the busiest in the area, however, although even busier than ever today, its role has long since changed. Until the construction of the Embankment some 200 years ago, this was part of the main eastern route out of Plymouth as the steep Lipson Hill presented all traffic with difficulties either going up - it was a challenge for any horse drawn carriage – or going down – coming down slowly wasn't always easy. Despite being long since eclipsed as the London road, however the junction has continued to get busier and busier, as reflected in the road widening and the installation of traffic lights. Clearly there have been other significant changes here too over the last 30 years: the late Victorian Beechwood factory (built as the Bedford Brewery and more recently known as Bowyers) disappeared in 1980 and after being twice hit during the Second World War and subsequently rebuilt and re-opened in 1954, St Augustine's Church has been completely demolished and the site is about to be redeveloped. *H 23 Feb 2008*

BRANDON ROAD

Take any two Now and Then domestic street scenes from anywhere around England separated by more than 40 years and the biggest single difference is almost certain to be in the number of cars on the road. Here, the seemingly quiet little backwater that is Brandon Road, Laira, is no different. A well-trodden route by those using the tunnel under the railway (near the former Laira Halt) the street and the houses, externally at least, look little changed, as does the visible part of the turn of the nineteenth-century board-school in Beverley Road, Laira Green - then an Infants, Juniors and Seniors mixed and now all Primary. Note also though, the disappearing sash windows and chimney pots.
H 21 Oct 2006

OLD LAIRA ROAD

The car population has grown spectacularly, the trees have grown significantly – although some street side specimens have been removed altogether and there has been the inevitable development of green spaces as Norfolk Road and Foxfield Close have been built behind the church of St Mary the Virgin, Laira. The church itself is now barely visible from this angle as the greenery has grown around it, but the stunted spire still punctures the skyline in the same way as it did when Dave Luckham took our delightful Then snap some 50 years ago (c.1960). Note the absence of street markings as well as the comparative lack of cars. Would that we had a view from 100 years ago, when the original Old Laira Road (formerly known as the Old London Road) dropped down beside the pub – the new, higher road, incidentally, was laid out in 1912.

LAIRA HALT

For a brief period, May 1848-April 1849, just after the railways had been extended as far west as Plympton, this was the next western most outpost. It was another 55 years before trains stopped here again as Laira Halt opened as a GWR station in June 1904 (never overly busy it was closed in July 1930). Situated close by the railway sheds, older residents will doubtless remember the railway men, with their clattery boots and grimy faces, who worked there before the diesel era came to the fore. Our Then picture is another of Trevor Lear's wonderful collection of Laira images from the late sixties and early seventies and while there have been plenty of changes – note the disappearing tracks - there are plenty elements common to both. *H 03 Jan 2007*

LAIRA TMD

The end of the steam train era spelt great changes for the Laira Railway Depot in 1964. The roundhouse and steam shed (built on reclaimed land on the edge of the Plym estuary at the beginning of the twentieth century) were closed the following summer – June 1965 - and removed soon afterwards. Trevor Lear's atmospheric Then photograph captures the scene shortly before the demolition men moved in. A new diesel shed had already been built to the south of the steam sheds at the beginning of the 1960s and the following decade a new long shed was built to service high speed trains – there were further adaptations to deal with the proposed servicing of Channel Tunnel sleeper trains, but the Plymouth to Paris service had yet to be introduced! Today Laira TMD – Traction Maintenance Depot – is nevertheless still busy and is currently administered by First Great Western. Comparing the two images, note the electricity pylon, the changes to the Mount Gould promontory and the disappearance of two sets of tracks in the foreground. *H 21 Apr 2007*

EMBANKMENT GARAGES

Thanks to Trevor Lear for this wonderful Seventies shot of the two garages that sat either side of the A374, on the approach to Marsh Mills, before the widening of the Embankment. Many will recall the old road prior to the creation of extra lanes inbound and outbound, following the infilling of the little tidal creek on the edge of the Plym. The Shell signs here consigned to the memory bank and old photo albums - with one garage grassed over (in front of the extended white house) and the other buried beneath the road - there is now a Texaco garage just visible behind the three-chevron slow-down warning, roughly where the old Crabtree Inn was. Note also the three outbound Austin motorcars - a reminder that not only was the road different then, but so was the type of traffic on it! *H 30 Sep 2006*

MANOR LANE

Sometimes it's easy to forget how things used to be when subtle changes are effected, like here at the bottom of Manor Lane. Although Embankment Road going into Plymouth Road has been greatly widened since our Then photograph was taken, you could be forgiven for thinking that the road had actually narrowed at this point, but in fact the access onto the road has just been moved slightly and in the process the garage here has disappeared – the building has gone and the entire forecourt area has been grassed over. Meanwhile a new outlet has been opened a 100 metres or so towards Marsh Mills. Other principal changes here over the almost 40-year period that separates these images are mainly concerned with car design, tree planting and tree growth, and the odd spot of domestic restructuring.. *H 06 Jan 2007*

CRABTREE INN

Thought to have been one of Plymouth's oldest inns, the Crabtree would have been a very popular resort for travellers crossing the Plym at the Ebb Ford (hence Efford) before the construction of the original Longbridge in the seventeenth century. Two hundred years later and the construction of the Embankment on the western bank of the Plym would have pushed yet further traffic past its door. However, as the roads improved and the amount of traffic on them increased relentlessly, so the old London Road became too narrow and in 1971 the Crabtree - and the neighbouring cottages - were pulled down to allow for the widening of the carriageway. *EH 14 Oct 2007*

RISING SUN

Some 200 hundred years ago the upstairs room of the old Rising Sun at Marsh Mills was known to one or two locals as the 'Crabtree Town Hall' and here the self-styled mayor of the cockle borough of Crabtree would receive the 'Great Cockle' along with his newly elected corporation. It was a popular and lively annual occasion but by the middle of the nineteenth century 'none cared to carry on the burlesque'. In the summer of 1973 (a few years after Trevor Lear captured our Then picture) the pub was renamed the Roundabout and in the summer of 1986 new developments at Marsh Mills Roundabout itself, prompted the closure and demolition of the pub. The area has since been redeveloped and a new hostelry stands to the east of this vantage point. *H 02 Jun 2007*

COLEBROOK, PLYMPTON.

COLEBROOK VILLAGE

The Chapel is largely obscured by its more recent neighbour, but is still clearly recognisable, as are a number of the other older properties here in the heart of Colebrook. What had been Farley's is now a Spar shop and two doors away from the store a two storey house has long since had a third floor added. Otherwise most of the chimney stacks still line up as do the two photographs, almost … your contemporary photographer is not so inclined to find the exact spot by standing in the middle of this now very busy road. One hundred years ago it was a different story and in order for our Then shot to have been taken, with no blurred human outlines, the figures captured here would have had to have held their pose for much longer than is sensible in such a location today. Motor vehicles of every kind now dominate this vista, along with the road markings and signage, which, as you can see suggest that this route is not suitable for general use by heavy vehicles. *H 19 Jan 2008*

COLEBROOK SHOPS

The commercial premises are little changed outwardly; the single-storey development beyond them has been replaced by a two-storey building; the low level structure fronting the street has disappeared, as has a window from the wall facing the camera. The chimney breast on the same property is lower and more narrow; the building beyond is much altered and trees now obscure the chapel. Telegraph poles carry more wires but remain in essentially the same positions, but a row of slim bollards now line the streetscape in front of the shops to prevent the unwanted intrusion of the motor car. Significantly our 'Then' image is car-free and the lack of double yellow lines suggests that motor vehicles were yet to be considered a problem here in Colebrook Road. How many more differences can you see in this fascinating pair of Plympton pictures? *H 01 Mar 2008*

THE RIDGEWAY

I can't think of another pavement in Plymouth that has shops along one side and a low wall running along part of the road line … with steps leading up to the street. Doubtless designed to stop vehicles falling off the road, thereby protecting pedestrians, it gives the ancient and narrow Ridgeway at Plympton a somewhat quirky flavour, a flavour that is enhanced by the variety of architectural styles, which in turn reflect the different ages of so many of the buildings that line this busy thoroughfare. Sadly the slate hanging has disappeared from the ground floor of the former Deeble's Electrical Store – now Job Centre Plus – but their electric clock ticks on, minus the Deebles sign, and the upper floor slates remain surmounted by the wonderfully detailed eves. Further up there have been yet more changes in the occupancy of these buildings since our Then image was taken – on 27 October 1980 – but the Plympton Conservative Club is still here: its signage may have altered, but its location has not. *H 02 Aug 2008*

RIDGEWAY No date on Roy Westlake's Then picture of the Ridgeway, but late-sixties would seem to be about right. At that time this was still a major Devon road, a far cry from the one-way pedestrian-friendly thoroughfare that it is today. Interestingly enough little appears to have changed on the northern side of the road, from this angle at least, while the skyscape and the south side of the street have changed dramatically. Gone now are the clutter of overhead telephone cables and gone too some of the open spaces behind the building line on this side of the street that formerly fronted the Methodist Chapel and the Police Station and Court House that were, in turn, built on the site of St Stephen's house which was demolished in 1935. Interestingly enough the new shopping precinct that has arisen in their place is known as St Stephen's. H 20 Oct 20076

FORE STREET, PLYMPTON ST MAURICE

Although the time separation between these two images isn't all that great – some 30 or 40 years – there wouldn't be a lot of difference if you wound the clock back 130 years or more. Indeed most, if not all, of these properties appear on Palmer's 1793 map of St Maurice and many, including the wonderful Guildhall building, had already been there for a hundred years and one or two since Tudor times. Notwithstanding all of that, there are of course subtle changes to be found: although there is no more room for parking today than there was when Roy Westlake took our Then image, there are invariably more cars around today; and while you barely notice the impact, visually, of small security alarm boxes on the outside walls of these houses, most now have them, thereby giving us another insight into the difference between the world of 40 years ago and today. *H 12 Jan 2008*

UNDERWOOD PLYMPTON

(Looking west) Comparing early photographs of local street scenes with current views of the same situation throws up many common themes, none more obvious than the impact that the motor car has made over the last 100 years. Here we see the Underwood of old, without a single wheeled-vehicle, of any description, in sight; a stark contrast with the same thoroughfare today, which is cluttered with cars at any time of night or day. The early telegraph pole too, makes its own statement about the passage of time – many more wires now hang from it, although we can but wonder how long it will be before we are all wire free. The buildings meanwhile, are much the same, although were any of them to be completely redeveloped in the modern smoke-free (well almost) world, then, like every other new development around the city, the new houses would almost certainly be chimney free. *H 23 Dec 2007*

UNDERWOOD PLYMPTON

One of the better-preserved areas of the city featuring significant blocks of old properties is, undoubtedly, Plympton and while St Maurice has perhaps the most photogenic collection of such attractions, there can be little doubt that the main thoroughfare through Underwood has its own comparatively timeless charm. Although Roy Westlake's period piece only takes us back some 30 or 40 years – when the Union Inn was still a Plymouth Breweries house – it is apparent that there has been a lot of 'modernisation' in the meantime. Old stonework facades have been rendered over, windows have been renewed, but, in most of this stretch, the narrowness of the road, and the ensuing necessity for double yellow lines, has prevented parked cars from providing the most obvious key to the passage of time – although the old Austin in the distance is a very rare sight today. *H 30 Dec 2007*

THE TIDE

The car in Trevor Lear's Then photograph is parked on the edge of the road, just opposite the erstwhile Crabtree Inn, while the car in our Now image is heading west along the fast-moving, three-lane approach road into the City from Marsh Mills, a road that, in the early 1970s, was constructed over this former inlet off the Plym. Known locally as 'The Tide', because its use was dependent on the state of the tide, we see it here at low tide. Between the old Plymouth Road and the waterline, on our right, on the original bank of the river, was the horse-drawn Plymouth and Dartmoor Railway; before the war the track and the surrounding foliage was often coated white with clay dust, much of it coming down from Lee Moor. *H 20 Jan 2007*

CHAPMAN'S GARAGE

A familiar enough view for anyone travelling into Plymouth along the Embankment but who remembers when Frank Chapman had a garage here? The back was supported on stilts and either side of the shop entrance at the front were a pair of Shell petrol pumps with the well-known shell-shaped motif at the top of each one. The trains thundered along at the back and the road junction was a lot more straightforward, a small roundabout channelling vehicles towards the city or off towards Mutley through Laira. The Embankment is much wider now and the turning off to Mutley dips under the main road and back up in the area of the original junction. Much busier now, you certainly wouldn't expect to find anyone walking their dog on the edge of the road these days. Back in the late sixties though, when Trevor Lear took our Then shot, this was a less hectic stretch. *H 30 Dec 2006*

TIDAL CREEK

Popularly known as 'the Tide' local children used to swim in there, but only at high tide: many of the boats that were kept in 'the Tide' could only get out at half tide – if the tide was too high they couldn't get under the arch of the railway bridge (that's the main line railway bridge) – but then the boatmen knew that: conversely if the tide dropped too far they couldn't get in because of the mud. A little over 30 years ago, all that came to an end though, with the infilling of the creek and the widening of the main road. Note the trees of Saltram reflected in Trevor Lear's Then picture, which was taken from a slightly lower vantage point, the road here having been built up so that the Mutley route could be diverted underneath the main thoroughfare. *H 27 Jan 2007*

LAIRA AVENUE

The gable end and chimney stack are the keys here: more radiantly white today the house in the middle of both photographs has not only had a fresh coat of paint but it has been extended significantly at the back. But there have been many other changes here too; the path here no longer disappears behind our vantage point under a bridge, rather the ground levels have been radically adjusted to cope with the widening of Embankment Road and the new Laira road junction. Meanwhile changes in the planting here variously reveal and conceal the changes in front of us as much of Laira Goods Yard is obscured by the modern growth and new housing. Careful examination of Trevor Lear's Then image allows us to see right into Laira Depot, but much of what we see Then is not there to be seen Now anyway, although this still is a major railway yard.
H 13 Jan 2007

DARTMOOR RAILWAY

When most of think of railways we tend also to think in terms of railway engines - steam, diesel, or electric – but not horse-powered, however the old Dartmoor Railway worked for many years in that way. Proposed formally by Sir Thomas Tyrwhitt, the man behind the construction of Dartmoor Prison, in 1919, it had been surveyed the previous year and was laid out in 1923. As it was older than the Great Western Railway line by a generation or so, its horse drawn traffic had priority over the steam trains at the Laira right up until 1960, even though latterly maybe only one train a year might use the crossing. Long gone now, the topography of the land around here is much altered and the bridge through which the horses have just pulled their load is now buried beneath the landfill that accompanied the widening of the Embankment roadway above and to the right - the houses to the left were all cleared around the same time. *EH 07 Oct 2007*

EGERTON PLACE

The date written alongside our then image of Egerton Place is April 9, 1959, and there's no reason to doubt its accuracy, which means that 50 years seperates these two fairly ordinary images. Ordinary but fascinating, the differences between the two provide an interesting insight into the cultural changes over that time: substantially fewer chimney stacks; the loss of the corner shop at the end of Anson Place (Edward Johnson had a boot and shoe repair business there in the fifties)'Ashman's butcher's shop (a little way down here on the left, in Egerton Place itself) and beyond it Simeon J Peters - baker. There is also the case of the disappearing telephone cables; the introduction of the pebble-dash house coat and the modern day parking restrictions... not to mention the odd house extension and window realignment. How many other differences can you spot? *EH 21 Mar 2009*

CATTEDOWN ROUNDABOUT

One of the interesting things about this Then and Now pairing from Richard Keoghoe is that you realise just how big Cattedown actually is. You notice, too, how seemingly random the planting on it is, and how sad it is that such a great green space cannot be used by members of the public (or anyone else for that metter), as there is no public access to it. Eighteen years have passed since Richard took his Then image and it's increasingly difficult now for anyone to remember those distant pre-roundabout, yet post-war days when Tothill Road used to extend right down past the junction with Cromwell Road to meet Embankment Road at a point not that far from where the three feather-duster-shaped trees have grown in the middle of what is a clearly-shaped circle on the right. *H 25 Jul 2009*

GDYNIA WAY

Thanks to Richard Keoghoe for this interesting pair of photographs; Richard found the Then image among some personal pictures he took when Gdynia Way had not all that long since been laid out along the line of the old railway route into Sutton Harbour. Here we look at right angles to that line, down from the pedestrian crossing below Cattedown Roundabout, across into Shapter's Road, at the back of Home Sweet Home Terrace, and out beyond that, curving around into Macadam Road. Richard thinks his Then image was taken around 1991 and is struck by the changes that have taken place here in the intervening years as we see in his Now image: the major new development off Cattedown Road on the left and the alterations to the landscape (right) since the gasometers have been reduced or removed. *H 25 Jul 2009*

ASTOR PLAYING FIELD A relatively unassuming Plymouth park today, the Astor Playing Fields off Embankment Road have an interesting history. Here it was that Plymouth Cricket Club played for over 40 years, between 1863 and 1905 (the club had been founded in 1857 and played their earliest games on the Hoe), Plymouth Rugby Club (founded in 1875 and the ancestor of Plymouth Albion) were also here for the last quarter of the nineteenth century, and into the twentieth century, and large crowds would often assemble to watch one or other. Other sports were also played here by local teams, however it's possible that perhaps the biggest crowd was in 1912 when 8,000 turned out to see an exhibition match of Northern Union Rugby, between Huddersfield and Oldham. The ground then was still known as South Devon Place, and held that name until Lord Astor bought it to ensure its future as a green space in 1917. Note the rear of the Methodist Church that sits on the edge of Cattedown Roundabout and the truncation of the terrace opposite (effected to make way for the roundabout).

LAIRA BRIDGE The biggest change is undoubtedly the disappearance of the Blue Circle Cement works which had only been open a few years when Laira Bridge first opened in 1961. For over 40 years it commanded its impressive vantage point only to be spectacularly demolished in 2001. Explosives were planted at two dozen points around the site and then deliberately detonated on a drizzly January morning, thereby bringing to an end an era whereby so many local buildings were built with local cement. The then new road bridge superseded the celebrated iron bridge - opened in 1828 it was one of the first in the country - but sadly only the end piers survive today. Meanwhile the road bridge looks much the same as it did in Roy Westlake's fascinating Then picture. There are plenty of other differences to spot too, foremost among them, the present use of this stretch of the Plym as a mooring for small leisure/pleasure craft. *H 13 Oct 2007*

POWER STATION

It doesn't seem all that long ago that the two tall chimneys of Plymouth 'B' power station pierced the skyline at the mouth of the Plym just below Laira Bridge, but then again up until 1973, Plymouth 'A' was still standing on the empty site we see alongside it. Wind the clocks back another generation, to 1948, and there will be some readers who can remember this area before Plymouth 'B' was built. Today, of course, the scene is transformed again and one wonders how long the existing landscape will survive and how long it will be before flats and housing are favoured over commercial use for this potentially very attractive piece of Plymouth waterfront. H 03 Nov 2007

POWER STATION

In 1948 work began on clearing the site for Plymouth's new power station. Constructed in two phases, one in 1953, the other in 1959, Plymouth 'B', initially planned as a coal-fired station, went over to oil with the completion of its second half in 1959. At that time the original coal-fired, Plymouth 'A' was still operating and there were some 300 people employed across the two plants. With the closure and demolition of the older plant in the 1970s that number was halved and less than a decade later 90% of the remaining workforce had gone as the newer station became a reserve unit. Soon afterwards it went altogether and in 2006 plans for a new gas-fired station at Langage were announced: meanwhile the waterfront continues to evolve in response to the demands of the day.
H 10 Nov 2007

POMPHLETT CREEK

With almost 50 years separating the two images undoubtedly the most obvious change here and at many other locations around the Plymouth area coastline, is change from a working waterfront to one dominated by the leisure and pleasure boat industry. Indeed it's hard to find any obvious common features apart from the basic topography, although look carefully enough and you see the long, low-gabled roof of what is now a prime Sugar Mill Estate building just to the right of centre on the other side of Billacombe Road. Many though, like Derek Carter, who supplied the 1960 image of Pomphlett Creek, will remember those days when the Everard ships came into the creek to be loaded up from the imposing, waterside, stone crushing plant; ships like the Sanguity here, which was built in Grangemouth in 1956 and scrapped (as the Romona) in 1994 in Brugges. *H 21 Jun 2008*

POMPHLETT MILL

Straddling Billacombe Brook, Pomphlett Mill had been in operation here since the sixteenth century at least and was owned and leased for most of that time by the Dukes of Bedford. In more recent times it was owned and operated by Billy Mitchell, who, with his brother Sidney, built Millway Terrace and Millway Place. The mill came down in the early 1960s (not long after Derek Carter took this photo), along with the three railway bridges and embankment behind the site (the best known of which was the one seen here on the left, over Billacombe Road), and the other at Stamp's Corner over Oreston Road. The railway used to service Oreston, Turnchapel and Hooe. Today the brook still filters through the site, and on the land on what would have been the other side of the tracks, is now a superstore, while a pedestrian route follows the line of the railway into Oreston. *H 07 Jun 2008*

ORESTON LANDING JETTY

The public pontoon in our Then photo (for which we thank Derek Carter of Oreston) was removed sometime around 1960. In its later years this pontoon could be accessed at more states of the tide than the old Oreston pontoon, which floated out from just in front of the King's Arms; consequently it was here that the P&O (Plymstock and Oreston) ferry used to pick up and drop off until the service stopped altogether. Today this is a private pontoon and the change is symptomatic of the bigger picture which has seen the closure and subsequent demolition of Plymouth's two electricity generating stations – Plymouth A and B – which stood for so many years on the other side of the river here. Increasingly this is a leisure and domestic based waterfront - the moored yachts, once a rarity, now a common feature of almost any sheltered stretch of estuary. *H 10 May 2008*

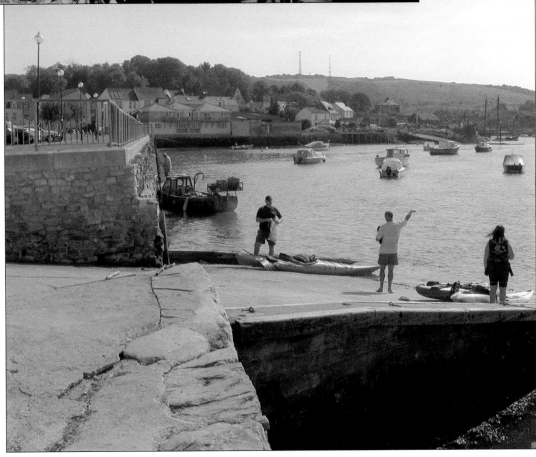

ORESTON

Almost 200 years ago Alexander Selkirk, the man who inspired Daniel Defoe to write 'Robinson Crusoe', married Frances Candish, the landlady of one of the four inns that once graced the Oreston waterfront. It was a decade or so after his four year ordeal on Juan Fernandez Island, in the South Pacific, and the year after Defoe's book was published – 1720. Doubtless he had many a tale of his own to tell. Selkirk appears not to have stayed here all that long however, despite his marriage, but he would have been here long enough to know this stretch of water well. In those days of course the water reached further inland, the former harbour having been infilled in the 1960s. The backdrop generally, though, has changed very little, although there would have been significantly fewer houses along the waterfront and none of those masts (which have now all but disappeared) above Mount Batten. *H 27 Oct 2007*

GREEN RAILINGS

The fascination for taking photographs of things that are about to be, or are in the process of being, demolished is nothing new, as this 50-year-old snap of 'Green Railings' and the adjoining cottages on the Oreston waterfront testifies. Quite why the double-gable-ended limestone building was known as Green Railings is uncertain, and although there's a suggestion it may have been a Customs and Excise building at one time, that doesn't seem to help explain anything. Whatever its history the complex was demolished in 1958 when Plympton Rural Council (amalgamation with Plymouth was still almost a decade away) decided to redevelop this and other bits of Oreston. Elford Drive was laid out soon afterwards and the King's Arms, just visible on the far right of both images, is one of the few remaining links between the two images. *H 18 Oct 2008*

ORESTON QUAY

The tide was out 50 years ago or more as we look back at our Then image from Derek Carter … and it's certainly out now as, for 40 years or so, the once bustling little inlet of the Plym has been infilled and grassed over. Note the old harbourside buildings straight ahead, that were then in the process of being demolished (interestingly enough these buildings had slate floors – on a high spring tide the water came in one door and went out the other!). Meanwhile those to the left survive today, although the corner property, which accommodated what was then Stibling's butcher's shop (the village slaughterhouse was at the back), has been dramatically converted in the loft department. Eady Philips' general store alongside, almost out of the picture, now forms part of the Plym Yacht Club, while over to the far right the discreet cross atop the gable end of the Church of the Good Shepherd is clearly visible in both pictures. *H 27 Sep 2008*

MARINE ROAD JUNCTION

There have been major changes in the street pattern here since the removal of the buildings that we see to the left of Derek Carter's Then image of the bottom end of Plymstock Road, Oreston. The building straight ahead fell to the bulldozers 50 years ago but many still remember it, along with the low granite set on the corner. Still to be seen on many an ancient street corner, these sets were there to force horse-drawn cartwheels away from the stonework to ensure that projecting wheel hubs did not damage the fabric of the building as the carts negotiated the tight turning. Note also the once-popular little corner shop on the opposite corner, and the more generous glimpse of the Plym afforded by the fact that the quay had yet to be infilled.
H 08 Nov 2008

ORESTON QUAY NORTH

A sea of green is what we now see as we look out across the erstwhile Quay at Oreston. It's not just the mud flats that have disappeared along with the Dummy – as the landing stage was known – several of the buildings have also long since gone; among them the large house to the right, in front of the tower as we see it, which went in the late-sixties around the time the quay was filled in, and Elford's warehouse just left of centre – the one-time home of a large threshing machine and a steam traction engine. In between the warehouse and the wall was 'Parliament Seat' where the old boys of the village would meet and sort out the problems of the world. Over to the left of Derek Carter's sixties shot we see the house known as Gutter End its great gable end still clearly visible today.

PARK LANE

The key building here, as we look down Park Lane, Oreston, is the old library cottage, the distinctive building in the centre of each image with the two brick-lined windows on the wall facing our vantage point. New building work on the other side of the church hall beyond that point, means that we only see the odd glimpse of the Plym from here now, what's more it's also difficult to fully appreciate the amount of change on the other side of the river as we peer through the foliage. On this side, in Derek Carter's Then image, the two nissen huts that served the World War II barrage balloon crew here are long gone, and the Orchard Crescent estate has been laid out on the erstwhile empty site, while Bayly's road is busier than ever as the approach to the new development off Hooe Lake around the Old Wharf. *H 14 Jun 2008*

PLYMSTOCK ROAD

Phone wires and television aerials now fill the skyline and the erstwhile farm looks less rustic than it did 40 or so years ago in this Derek Carter photograph, and it's many more years since there were animals on the farm. Long gone too are the old cottages in this stretch of Plymstock Road, Oreston; the new premises here now set back from the road. However there is still a visible 'v' shaped repair in the stonework of the wall jutting out into the road on the right. It was Wilf Tope's horse, Prince, that made the hole when he charged down the road, milk cart behind him, in a blind panic after a cover had blown off a nearby pram and landed on the horse's head. Note also how the scene is still comparatively car free, but only on account of the narrowness of the thoroughfare and, of course, the double yellow lines. *H 11 Oct 2008*

BROADWAY

It's a long time since the old market garden at Plymstock gave way to the mid-sixties development we now know as the Broadway. The fire station and neighbouring garage were first and when Roy Westlake's Then picture was taken there was still a bus stop opposite the tunnel alongside Woolworth's. It was, of course, pedestrianised a few years after that and now wooden horses and furniture provide a leisure area in the middle of what had been a busy traffic route. But the changes are not just confined to street furniture and traffic arrangements, there has been a steady changeover of occupants of the various retail outlets and where we saw Victoria Wine, Dingles, Millbay Laundry, Widgers and Fine Fare, we now see the Card Bar, Jag mobile phones, Specsavers, Select and Somerfields – changes which in themselves tell us a lot about the changes in our own lifestyles over the last 30 or 40 years.
H 05 Jan 2008

TURNCHAPEL SWING BRIDGE

The railway line into Turnchapel, a branch of the London and South Western Railway, opened in 1897 and a passenger service operated across this point for the next 50 years or so. The curious swing bridge over the entrance to Hooe Lake was formerly operated manually by the signalman from the Turnchapel Signal Box. Opened to allow boats in and out of the lake, the signalman would be stranded until he had hand-cranked the bridge back into position. In September 1951 the regular passenger service stopped, however the bridge continued to be used for another ten years or so and our Then photograph, from Derek Carter, shows a Railway Circle Special train crossing the old structure on the 30 September 1961. H *25 Oct 2008*

HOOE LAKE SWINGBRIDGE

It was on 2 October 1961 that the Turnchapel signal box closed for the last time, Plymouth Railway Circle's last tour of the line having taken place just a couple of days earlier on 30 September. For 64 years the line into Turnchapel had been open, Turnchapel Station being located just yards from the bridge on the opposite side of Hooe Lake as we look across it here. Two years later, in October 1963, work began on the demolition of the swing bridge since when it has looked pretty much as it does today, the great tubular supports standing as solid silent reminders of that bygone era when steam trains connected the country in a way many wish would return. *H 29 Oct 2008*

BORINGDON ROAD, TURNCHAPEL Forty years separate the two images and while there is at first glance temptation to think that everything is much the same, there has actually been a lot of change in this little corner of Turnchapel. The new-build on the right is perhaps the most obvious example, but there are other more subtle differences. One by one chimney stacks have been replaced by satellite dishes as fireside chats have given way to more impersonal televisual diversions; a street light has appeared as the population of the village has increased and behind us the new Clovelly View development has appeared, while furthest from the camera we see what was then Starkey, Knight & Ford's New Inn is now the Clovelly Bay Inn (the area looks out over Clovelly Bay) an enlarged and much enhanced hostelry. The figure in the foreground, incidentally, is Derek Carter, the man took the Then photograph back in 1968. *H 05 Jul 2008*

HEXTON HILL We're a little bit further up the hill than Derek Carter was in 1963 when he took this Then shot looking down Hexton Hill Road. The main telling point is the relationship between the skyline and the chimney pot of the Royal Oak pub, whose sign we see quite clearly in the older image. Back then, of course, Hooe Lake still ran up beyond the pub right up to Hooe Road. Since the mid-sixties however it has been filled in almost in line with the pub; although the delightfully named Yonder Street still runs to the right from the bottom of Hexton hill around part of the lake's edge. H 12 Jul 2008